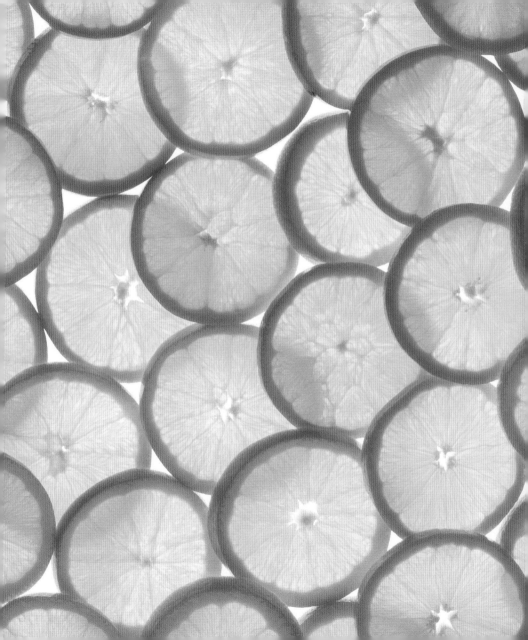

DUMONT'S LEXICON OF

HERBAL REMEDIES

Ingredients • Medical Effects • Application

Anne Iburg

**Photographs by
Roland Spohn**

REBO
PUBLISHERS

© 2004 Rebo International b.v., Lisse, The Netherlands

Text: Anne Iburg
Photographs: Roland Spohn
Typesetting: AdAm Studio, Prague, The Czech Republic
Cover design: AdAm Studio, Prague, The Czech Republic

Translation: Tomáš Svoboda for Agentura Abandon, Prague,
The Czech Republic
Proofreading: Emily Sands, Jeffrey Rubinoff, Eva Munk

ISBN 90 366 1691 3

Contents

Introduction

The use of plant-based remedies has become a well-established part of modern medicine. Treating ailments with medicinal plants stimulates the body's defense system so that the body essentially deals with the malady itself, thus representing a holistic approach. One ought to keep in mind, however, that not everyone's self-healing ability reacts the same or is sufficiently stimulated by herbal treatments. Natural medicine might not be powerful enough for each and every ailment and is not necessarily suitable for every person.

THE HISTORY OF NATURAL MEDICINE

The history of natural medicine goes back to the very roots of mankind. For thousands of years, people all over the world have been gathering plants not only for food, but also as cures for illness and injury. This age-old empirical knowledge has been passed from generation to generation, right up to our current day.

The Egyptians were a people who made great use of the healing power of plants. One of the oldest surviving records of natural medicine is the Papyrus Ebers, which was written as early as 1500 BC on the banks of the Nile and is now kept at the library of the

University of Leipzig in Germany. The compendium is 20 meters long and contains information on more than 500 natural ingredients in more than 800 recipes. The reader learns, for example, that dropsy was treated with squill, radishes were used in pectoral medicine and garlic and onion were regarded as "natural antibiotics."

Ramses II reportedly employed a staff of physicians, with each individual in charge of a particular disease pattern. At about the same time the pyramids were built, Egypt saw the establishment of a number of herbalism schools. Good medical care was not only available to kings; the lower classes also profited from the knowledge of how to prevent and alleviate illness. For example, the construction workers who built the pyramids were given food mixed with medicinal herbs to protect them from epidemic diseases.

Landscape gardening in ancient Egypt

Herbal medicine in ancient Greece

Herbal medicine had its heyday in ancient Greece in the days of Hippocrates (460–370 BC), who, in his treatise "Corpus Hippocraticum" describes, among other things, more than 230 medicinal plants. Hippocrates' family claimed descent from the demigod Asklepios - son of Apollos, the healing god. It is said that, following the family tradition, Hippocrates was introduced in his childhood years to the uses and effects of medicinal plants by his father, Heracleidas. Later, he traveled around Greece and Asia Minor in order to practice and further develop his medical expertise. A famous and respected man, he returned to the island of Kos to practice medicine, write treatises and teach medical students at his own school.

Aristotle (384–322 BC) wrote a book on botany and another Greek, Claudius Galenus of Pergamon, a.k.a. Galen (129–199 AD), medical attendant to the Roman emperor Marcus Aurelius, compiled a list of all medicinal plants known at the time into a comprehensive volume with detailed instructions for preparation and use. His word remained the authority on the subject throughout the Middle Ages.

The five-volume *Materia Medica* by Pedanius Dioscorides (40-90 AD) was the key work on medicinal plants of the ancient world. Written in the first century AD, it details more than a thousand medicinal treatments involving plants, animals and minerals. As late as the 16th century, it was still the reference of choice for anyone interested in medicinal plants. Dioscorides came from Anazarbus (Caesarea) in Cilicia, located in what is now called Turkey. In the preface to his opus magnum, he describes himself as a military doctor on the payroll of the Roman legions.

Dioscurides

What is intriguing about *Materia Medica* is that some of its empirical findings on the effects and toxicity of substances have been verified by modern science. Examples are the analgesic potential of the opium poppy, the use of peppermint to treat headaches and the astringent effects of oak and willow.

Greek physicians in ancient Rome

While there were a number of practicing physicians in ancient Rome, the majority of Romans brought their health concerns to gods of healing, such as Aesculap. Only the rich could afford the treatment provided by learned Greek physicians. Military doctors took care of those wounded and injured in combat, but not civilian patients. Most Roman medications were based on plants – Pliny the Elder described hundreds of plants renowned for their preventive or curative effects. Most ointments and medicines contained herbs such as sage, rosemary and fennel as well as vegetables such as cabbage, garlic, onion and leek. Roman soldiers received a daily ration of garlic to stay healthy and fit for upcoming battles.

A new perception of illness

During the great period of migration, the lore of medicinal plants began to fade. Those suffering from diseases were increasingly ostracized because people believed diseases were a form of punishment by the gods inflicted upon victims due to their sin. The spread of Christianity, however, engendered a different perception of diseases. For the good Christian, helping the poor, the weak and the ill was part of following the example of Jesus Christ. Medical care was often part of the agenda of religious orders, not to mention the monasteries which recorded the medicinal effects of plants. Monks and nuns formed part of the educated class of society and by drawing links between the knowledge of ancient Greece and the folklore of their contemporaries, they developed a medical science in its own right.

Wise women and witches

Traditionally, those who were later considered "witches" were, for the most part, midwives and wise women. Knowing the effects of various plants and herbs, they were able to help people in all sorts of curative ways. Nearly every village had its own wise woman and midwife, whose opinions were much respected and valued. These women gave advice in cases of illness and tended to expectant mothers during labor, birth and childbed.

The German word for witch, "Hexe," derives from the Old High German phrase, "Hagazussa," or "she who sits on the hedge." This reflects the once widespread belief that hedges not only separate one plot of land from another, but also separate this world from the supernatural world of trolls, pixies and other spirits. Thus, "she who sits on the hedge" was someone able to move between and communicate with both worlds.

The witches' knowledge and the power associated with it were a thorn in the flesh of the powerful and mighty at the time. The clergy and the nobility instigated malicious rumors about witches, thus preparing the ground for their persecution, the proverbial 'witch hunt.'

Monastic medicine

St. Benedict (the founder of the monastic order of the Benedictines) and his friar, Cassiodor, were especially concerned with tending to those suffering from illness. The training of monks as medical experts and nursing staff was possible thanks to St. Benedict's instructions. Cassiodor was in charge of the practical implementation of the new science; he founded a monastic academy that taught, among other subjects, herbal medicine.

Medieval monastery garden

Natural medicine became widespread under the reign of Charlemagne in the 8th century AD. Monasteries aimed at being self-sufficient, often growing medicinal plants next to edible fruits and vegetables in their gardens. The network of religious orders brought Mediterranean plants over the Alps and introduced them to Central Europe.

The abbess Hildegard von Bingen lived in the days of King Frederick Barbarossa, who was among those she advised in medical matters. Her approach to curing illnesses was holistic: both the body and the soul need to be cured, not just the immediately affected part of the body. She believed that the individual human is part of a larger network and is connected to all creation through metaphorical twigs and branches. Her medical book is a comprehensive treatise on both faith and natural philosophy, maintaining that a healthy way of life, proper nutrition and medicinal plants all have roles to play in maintaining health. She compiled both the knowledge of her order and the folk wisdom of the peasants, producing a vast literary output until her death in 1179.

Paracelsus was the founding father of modern herbal medicine. After his medical studies in Ferrara, Italy, the physician, pharmacist, natural philosopher and theologian, Paracelsus, a.k.a. Theophrastus Bombastus von Hohenheim (1493–1541), traveled all over Europe before settling in Basel, Switzerland. Conflicts with the local faculty made him flee to Austria, where he settled in Salzburg. His work "Herbarius" marks the beginning of a systematization of domestic natural medicine. He attempted to separate the essence of plants, which he called "arcanum," from their useless components in order to produce entirely pure agents. He thus obtained the first tinctures - distilled plant extracts in alcohol. According to his philosophy, "all things are poison and nothing is without poison. It is the dosage that makes a thing poisonous."

Father Kneipp and stepping water

In the 19th century, Father Sebastian Kneipp achieved worldwide recognition as an amateur healer in natural medicine. His publications, including "My Water Cure" and "Thus Thou Shalt Live," brought him worldwide fame almost overnight. Father Sebastian Kneipp took a natural, holistic approach to healing. Under his method, many ailments can be cured, resistance to disease can be strengthened and good health can be maintained, all by following simple advice relating to plenty of light, fresh air, water, exercise, relaxation, purification and a natural diet.

GRANDMA'S HOUSEHOLD REMEDIES

Household remedies for colds, coughs, sore throats, upset stomachs or diarrhea were usually recipes exchanged within the family and passed on to the next generation by the matriarch. The modern nuclear family places little importance on such traditions and if we seek help in medical matters, we go to a doctor. In such an environment, the older generations are no longer able to pass on their expertise to others. However, if you are interested in household remedies, you should not hesitate to ask the elderly for counsel – some pieces of their advice are invaluable and you will most likely encounter such wisdom in the course of this book.

HOMEOPATHY

After decades of research, the physician and founder of homeopathy, Samuel Hahnemann (1755–1843), succeeded in developing an independent healing method based upon his observations of nature. His method has endured to the present day and is based on the following principles: 'like cures like,' the art of handpicking an appropriate cure, and the choice of a proper dilution (potency ratio).

Such a method is rooted in two of Hahnemann's observations, made over the course of his experimental studies. Firstly, healthy individuals who take medicine develop symptoms very similar to pathological symptoms; secondly, 'like cures like;' i.e. substances that incur similar symptoms in healthy individuals are the cure of choice for the pathological symptoms of patients. For example, a healthy stomach will respond to chamomile with cramps; therefore, chamomile is apt to alleviate the pains caused by an upset stomach.

Disclaimer:

Phytotherapy, or 'plant medicine' in the language of experts, is but one segment of homeopathy, albeit a very significant one. Even someone with great expertise in plant-based medicine is far from being competent enough to attempt homeopathic self-medication. This requires extensive knowledge and experience, which is why we advise against self-medication with homeopathic drugs.

PHYTOTHERAPY TODAY

The study and practice of phytotherapy has grown far beyond the limits of purely empirical science. While plant medicine was at first marginalized by modern medicine due to a climate of increasing faith in technology and to the availability of synthetic drugs, it has now found new recognition. One reason is that modern scientific analysis allows us to isolate specific active ingredients in plants and identify their properties. Moreover, these studies show the curative effect that such ingredients can have on certain medical conditions. This said, however, some medicinal plants contain many as yet unidentified substances. This lack of full knowledge regarding unknown elements in medicinal plants can be either viewed as a positive or negative thing, depending on the individual scientist's attitude towards natural medicine – specifically, plant medicine.

Those with a positive attitude claim that the unknown substances, in interaction with active ingredients already known, harbor especially great potential for healing diseases. This claim is based on the optimistic view that Mother Nature's pharmacy has better medicines in stock than those produced by man – whether synthetically or based on plant extracts. The more critical voices object on the grounds that that it might be dangerous to prescribe substances which have not been fully researched and which contain substances with unknown effects. The latter school would rather opt for clearly defined compounds. In this regard, one may point out that human beings are a part of nature just as much as plants and it is impossible for every detail to be known in full.

There exist two antithetical schools and yet natural medicine and so-called "conventional medicine" have already converged a great deal. Natural medicines enjoy more recognition than ever and open-minded, educated patients are calling for a mix of natural medicine and conventional medicine. Most practitioners have responded favorably to this trend.

SELF-MEDICATION WITH MEDICINAL PLANTS

Women in general are more willing to try and use medicinal plants. They trust their perception of their bodies and rely on earlier experiences with medicinal plants. They attempt to cure their ailments by natural means, instead of consulting the doctor right away.

Medicinal plants are primarily used to fight coughs and the common cold. Peppermint and sage, as well as hot milk with honey, are popular household remedies for these complaints. Lime-tree flowers and elder are traditionally used to reduce fevers. Provided that the illness has only recently set in and the symptoms respond positively to self-treatment, nothing can be said against such an approach. Still, lasting illnesses with no signs of improvement warrant a doctor's visit. Digestive problems, nervousness and kidney problems also respond well to plant therapy. Moreover, many medicinal plants contain a number of compounds that may have beneficial effects on heart problems and cancer. However, one must not overestimate the power of medicinal plants. In most cases, even though they are unable to cure more serious medical conditions, herbal remedies can only complement more conventional therapies.

IMPORTANT ACTIVE INGREDIENTS

Many of the active substances contained in medicinal plants have been described by science, but many more compounds are still unknown. It is commonly accepted that the effects of the isolated compounds will not be identical to the integrated effects of the plant as a whole. This is one reason why the use of medicinal plants continues to be introduced cautiously into modern, evidence-based medicine, but only when the active agents can be identified. The following is a brief overview of the most important known active ingredients.

▬ ESSENTIAL OILS
More than 100 individual substances are categorized as essential oils. They all share common traits, e.g., they have anti-inflammatory effects on irritated skin, facilitate expectoration, are diuretics and anticonvulsants and have a tonic effect on the stomach, intestines, liver and gallbladder.

▬ ALKALOIDS
This is a group of very potent agents, also referred to as "curative toxins." Plants containing alkaloids as a main ingredient should only be used for medicinal purposes, other than external application, with a doctor's supervision. One well-known alkaloid is atropine, contained in high concentrations in belladonna, commonly known as deadly nightshade. A dose of

Fennel seeds contain essential oils

0.5 mg of this psychoactive agent is enough to cause psychomotor unrest, confusion, talkativeness and major rage attacks. Belladonna is thus not suitable for self-medication.

In small doses, however, and as a supportive ingredient in synergic combination with other ingredients, alkaloids can have a positive impact on the healing powers of plants. In general, they have vasopressive, excitatory and anticonvulsant effects.

▬ BITTERS

The acidic taste of many medicinal plants is caused by bitters. These substances principally fall into three groups. The first one facilitates the production of gastric juice and has tonic effects. The second group are produced in connection with essential oils. They have antiseptic effects and stimulate secretion in the intestines, liver and gallbladder. The third group is also known as capsaicinoids. They are rare in European plants, but are found in ginger, pepper and galangal, and they stimulate digestion and cardiovascular functions.

Gentian contains bitters

▬ FLAVONOIDS

Flavonoids are a very broad group of plant constituents with similar chemical structures. Today we know of more than 5,000 different flavonoids. They do not have uniform effects: one group of flavonoids improves the flexibility of the smallest blood vessels, the capillaries; another group helps against cramps in the gastrointestinal tract and another influences the cardiovascular system. Flavonoids also enhance the effects of other plant constituents.

▬ TANNINS

Tannins are plant constituents which are able to bind proteins in skin and mucous membranes, rendering them more resistant. Tannins are astringent and help to kill the bacteria that settle on injured skin and mucous membranes.

▬ GLYCOSIDES

The glycoside group is also very large, with a broad range of varied effects. Their most common trait is that they can be decomposed by hydrolysis (the presence of water) or with enzymes. One well-known glycoside is digitalis, contained in foxglove, which has potent cardiac effects. Other glycosides primarily influence the gastrointestinal tract.

Blackberry leaves contain tannins

▬ SILICA

Silicic acid, or silica (as it is more commonly called in its crystalline form) facilitates healthy connective tissue, hair and nails. In high doses, silicic acid is a diuretic.

▬ SAPONINS

Saponins liquefy mucus and thus facilitate expectoration. They have an antibiotic effect, invigorate the immune system and have a similar composition to glycosides.

▬ MUCILAGE

Mucilage is a type of substance that is rich in carbohydrates, capable of swelling in water, and stringy or slimy in consistency. Mucilage has a soothing effect.

▬ MUSTARD OILS

Mustard oils belong to the essential oils category. They have a spicy taste, stimulate the gastrointestinal tract and are highly antibiotic.

▬ VITAMINS

Provitamin A, or betacarotene, stabilizes the body's immune system and promotes cell regeneration. Group B vitamins play a key role in the metabolism of energy. Vitamin C contributes to invigorating the immune system and strengthens the body's defenses.

▬ MINERAL SUBSTANCES

In terms of quantity, potassium is the most representative mineral substance in natural medicine. High doses of potassium are diuretic. Some plants are rich in calcium and magnesium, which are both important for the metabolism of bones.

VARIOUS USES OF MEDICINAL PLANTS

▬ OIL

Medicinal plant oils are usually based on olive oil. Dried herbs are preferable over fresh plants, as the latter tend to go rancid quickly. One should also bear in mind that, during the extraction of healing substances, the preparation is to be shaken once per day and after the extraction, the mixture must be strained. Medicinal plant oils should be prepared in small amounts and stored in opaque bottles. They are primarily made for external use.

■ Powder
Grinding dried plants creates powder, which should only be taken internally if one desires the herbs to work especially fast. Otherwise, herb powder can be added to ointments and pastes and used externally.

■ Tincture
Tinctures are alcoholic extracts usually made from preparations of alcohol with fresh plants. Pharmaceutical alcohol may be substituted with schnapps, vodka or other spirits. After two to six weeks, the preparation is strained and should be stored in a cool, dark place. Tinctures are either diluted or taken in drops.

■ Decoction
Decoctions are prepared through a process of slowly boiling plants in water. Steep for no longer than ten minutes, then strain.

■ Infusion
Infusions represent the classic way of preparing tea. Pour hot water over the medicinal plants and

steep for (in most cases) no longer than ten minutes. Strain and sweeten with honey or sugar, according to purpose and taste.

▬ Cold extraction
For a cold extraction, the medicinal plant is covered with cold water and left to soak for a period of time, usually one day, in order to extract the active constituents. Stir occasionally. As a rule, the residue is not squeezed out after straining.

▬ Juice
Juices are produced from the fresh plant by squeezing the fruit, leaves or roots. If they are to be consumed primarily for their vitamin content, they should be prepared fresh and consumed immediately.

▬ Syrup
Syrups are thick solutions, which are prepared using juices or herb preparations made with water or wine, and are thickened by cooking with sugar.

▬ Ointment
Ointments are for external use only. The basis for ointments is usually medicinal oil, which is heated up and hardened with wool fat (lanolin) and beeswax.

▬ Baths
Whether it be a full bath, sitz bath, footbath or handbath: the basis for all is herbs or herb extracts,

highly diluted with hot water. Baths serve primarily for external use, though to some degree, volatile substances are inhaled (see Vapor baths, below). The main principle of baths is the supply of active substances in combination with heat, which warms up the entire body (or the affected area) and encourages relaxation and relief from ailments.

▬ VAPOR BATHS (INHALATION)
Volatile substances are released into the rising water vapor during a hot bath containing specific herbs or herb extracts. These are mostly used for treating respiratory ailments and are renowned for having healing and cosmetic effects on the skin.

▬ WET PACKS AND POULTICES
Warm packs and poultices (fomentation) are used to alleviate tension, muscle pain or skin diseases. Conversely, gauze wrappings soaked with tinctures create a cooling effect, which is used to minimize pain associated with bruises, mild burns or inflammations.

COLLECTING AND STORING MEDICINAL PLANTS

There is no definitive answer to the principled and recurring debate of whether herbs should be collected from nature, grown on one's own or bought at a pharmacy. The less confident or knowledgeable one

is regarding medicinal plants, the more one should rely on the professional opinion of a pharmacist. If you happen to have a green thumb, you might want to try growing medicinal plants at home, especially since most of them are easy to grow. If you prefer to collect herbs in the wilderness, you must always be able to identify a prospective plant. If you aren't completely able to, it is better not to pick the plant.

COLLECTING MEDICINAL PLANTS

The primary decision is where to collect herbs. Do not choose locations near roads with heavy traffic, popular dog-walking areas or heavily fertilized fields. Collecting protected plants (such as arnica in parts of Europe) is prohibited; in natural reserves and wildlife sanctuaries, this prohibition may extend to all flora, so make sure to check with the relevant local authorities first. Do not pick the entire stock in any given location: leave at least a third of the plants untouched, especially if it is a rare species. Of course, feel free to collect as much nettle and dandelion as you wish – they are sturdy plants and reproduce abundantly.

The right circumstances for collecting medicinal plants are a matter of expertise. It is, however, generally inadvisable to collect them in bad weather, as it is harder to process wet plants. Flowers should be plucked individually; alternatively, cut the flower as a whole. The concentration of active substances is the highest immediately after blooming.

Big leaves should be plucked individually, but smaller leaves can be collected by the stem and stripped later. The younger the leaf is, the higher its concentration of active substances.

The herb as a whole should be cut off just above the ground. Remove the woody, hardened parts before or after drying the herb.

Fruit should be picked at their peak of ripeness. If they come in umbels (as in elder), cut off as a whole and, at home, strip berries from stems.

Roots must be dug out, cleaned of soil and thoroughly washed. Collectors of herbal roots should ensure they harvest only a small part of the plant, leaving the rest undamaged.

If you are on a collecting tour for several medicinal plants, make sure you transport them separately, but not in plastic bags. Emerging humidity cannot escape from plastic bags and is the ideal nutrient medium for the development of fungi. Paper bags, linen bags or baskets are recommended.

PROPER DRYING AND STORAGE

Medicinal plants should be stored in airy and dry places such as attics. Whole herbs can be loosely bundled in bouquets and suspended from a line. It is best to dry flowers and leaves on a linen cloth or paper, with sufficient spacing, which requires a lot of room. Roots ought be dried in the oven at 120°F or on a well-heated radiator.

Dry herbs may be kept in paper bags, cloth pouches, tins, wooden cases or glass jars in dry places and away from light. Label the containers and refill them only with the same plant to avoid mixing aromas.

As a rule, medicinal herbs can be stored for one to two years. When they lose their scent, appear a dull color or crumble easily, they are outdated and no longer contain active substances.

GROWING YOUR OWN MEDICINAL PLANTS

To some extent, you can grow medicinal plants in a garden or on a balcony. The following plants are suitable for establishing an herb garden:

ANNUAL AND BIENNIAL PLANTS
Watercress, fumitory, chamomile, caraway, parsley, marigold, mustard, sunflower, yellow sweet clover, viola

PERENNIALS
Field horsetail, arnica, valerian, comfrey, burnet, tormentil, nettle, ivy, lady's mantle, silverweed, hops, coltsfoot, St. John's wort, dandelion, balm, mint, agrimony, rosemary, sage, yarrow, English plantain, thyme

SELF-MEDICATION AND ITS LIMITS

Whether to treat ailments yourself or whether to consult a doctor is your choice. There are pros and cons to either approach:

■ ARGUMENTS FOR SELF-MEDICATION
• You know the limits of your skills and will see a physician before it is too late.
• You know your body well enough to be able to render a self-diagnosis.
• You feel confident enough in handling household remedies to differentiate between the various herbs and to administer their proper doses.
• For each symptom, there are a variety of household remedies to which different people will respond differently. You have the critical self-awareness to realize whether a chosen remedy works for you.
• You have the self-confidence to see your doctor if self-medication fails and to report your unsuccessful efforts accurately.
• You do not consider household remedies a universal remedy or panacea. You are a critical – indeed, self-critical – individual, who is ready to admit mistakes.

▄▄▄ ARGUMENTS AGAINST SELF-MEDICATION

• You are unsure whether this household remedy really cures your ailments.

• You find it difficult to attribute your symptoms to a specific medical condition, as they are too ambiguous. You cannot arrive at a diagnosis by yourself.

• You are unsure of the proper identification of the household remedy you are considering using.

• You are afraid of or want to avoid seeing a doctor.

• You recurringly suffer from the same symptoms, without knowing their cause.

• You don't really believe yourself capable of self-treatment, but you want to save time and money.

Yarrow

Achillea millefolium

■ SYNONYMS: milfoil, bloodwort

■ PARTS USED: The flowers and leaves of yarrow are used. The main active ingredients are essential oils, bitters, tannins, flavonoids, salicylic acid, sequiterpenes and potassium.

■ MEDICINAL EFFECTS: The essential oils relieve intestinal cramps, soothe stomachache and fight inflammations. The flavonoids have antibiotic effects. Salicylic acid alleviates pain and sesquiterpenes and potassium reduce the propensity for edema.

IMPORTANT NOTE

Certain people respond to skin contact with yarrow with a local allergic reaction. These individuals should avoid yarrow in any form as a household remedy.

■ APPLICATIONS: Yarrow tea relieves abdominal cramps caused by menstruation or by poor eating habits. A tea regimen has diuretic effects and prevents edema. The regimen is also recommended for gout patients. Furthermore, yarrow tea is said to stimulate blood circulation. Used externally, a yarrow poultice helps with minor burns and open wounds and facilitates the healing process. A sitz bath is said to alleviate hemorrhoids; footbaths supposedly stimulate blood circulation and thus alleviate vein problems. A full bath is said to relieve cramps and have soothing effects on pains associated with rheumatism, gout and neuroses.

Tea:

Pour 1 cup hot water over 1 teaspoon yarrow, steep for approximately ten minutes, then strain. Do not consume more than 2 cups per day. A yarrow regimen should be observed over six weeks, followed by a 4-week break.

Tea mixture for improved blood circulation:

Mix 2 teaspoons yarrow with 1 teaspoon hawthorn. Pour 2 cups boiling water over the mixture. Steep for fifteen minutes, then strain. Drink lukewarm.

Poultice:

Pour 2 cups boiling water over 1 handful of yarrow. Immerse a linen or gauze cloth in the decoction and place on the wound while still warm.

Bath:

For a sitz bath or footbath, pour 2 cups boiling water over 1 handful yarrow and allow to soak for several hours. Strain decoction and add to hot bathwater. For a full bath, double the amount. Bathe for ten minutes.

Horse chestnut

Aesculus hippocastanum

■ SYNONYMS: conker, Spanish chestnut

PARTS USED: The seeds (and occasionally the leaves, flowers and bark) of the chestnut tree are used. The most potent ingredients are aescin, tannins and flavonglycosides.

■ MEDICINAL EFFECTS: The active ingredients have a strong effect on blood vessels, particularly veins, relieving cramps and soothing pain.

■ APPLICATIONS: Using horse chestnut tinctures or applying a swathe with horse chestnut paste is said to alleviate vein problems and rheumatism. Such swathes are also said to alleviate gastrointestinal maladies. The paste can be applied to hardened breasts to speed up healing of inflammations. A sitz bath in horse chestnut decoction helps with hemorrhoids. Tea from horse chestnut leaves is often recommended as a mucolytic tea for coughs.

DID YOU KNOW ...

Superstition has it that carrying 3 horse chestnuts in your pocket will protect you from diseases of all kinds.

TEA:

Pour 1 cup boiling water over 1 rounded teaspoon dried horse chestnut leaves; steep for ten minutes, then strain. Sweeten with honey.

SITZ BATH / FOOTBATH:

Pour 1 cup boiling water over 2 rounded tablespoons of chestnut flour and crushed chestnut leaves; steep for ten minutes, then strain. Place in sitz bath and bathe for ten minutes. If applied as a footbath, add 1 tablespoon of thyme leaves.

TINCTURE:

Pour ½ cup brandy over 2 tablespoons chestnut flour and 2 tablespoons crushed chestnut leaves; seal well. Steep for 2 weeks, then strain. Pour into an opaque, sterile, sealable flask. Rub into joints, lower legs or upper body, as needed.

PASTE:

Mix horse chestnut flour 1:1 with wheat flour, add vinegar and mix until thick. Apply to affected areas or spread in thin layer on gauze and wrap around aching areas.

Agrimony

Agrimonia eupatoria

■ SYNONYMS: cocklebur, sticklewort

PARTS USED: The whole herb is used. The main active ingredients are triterpenes, tannins, bitters, flavonoids, silicic acid and mucilage.

■ MEDICINAL EFFECTS: The tannins contribute to the healing of wounds and alleviate pain, since they bind water upon direct contact with the tissue and thus deprive germs of their nutritional basis. The bitters stimulate increased secretion of mucus. The flavonoids and the triterpenes have anticonvulsant and antibiotic effects.

■ APPLICATIONS: Agrimony tea helps with diarrhea and with gastrointestinal diseases. It stimulates production of gastric juice and bile. Gargling with agrimony tea helps sore throats and fights pharyngitis. Tinctures are said to be very effective and are popular among professional singers and orators. Footbaths of agrimony are said to soothe ailing feet.

DID YOU KNOW ...

Agrimony is widespread in northern and Central Europe as well as in North America, and we help it to spread without noticing: the fruit is equipped with little hooks which attach easily to clothes.

Tea:

Pour 1 cup boiling water over 1 rounded teaspoon dried agrimony and strain after ten minutes. May also be used for gargling when cool.

Gargle/tincture:

Pour ½ cup brandy over 4 tablespoons dried agrimony and soak for approximately 2 weeks in a warm, dark place. Strain and pour into a sterile, opaque bottle. Gargle with 1 tablespoon tincture to half a glass water.

Footbath:

Mix tablespoons dried agrimony with 5 tablespoons dried sage and 5 tablespoons dried marigold. Pour 1 quart boiling water over the mixture and steep for ten minutes. Pour decoction into foot tub, dilute with lukewarm or cold water until the water is a good temperature and add 2 tablespoons cider vinegar. Bathe feet in water for ten to 20 minutes, rub dry and apply oily foot lotion.

Lady's Mantle
Alchemilla vulgaris

▬ SYNONYMS: lion's foot, stellaria

▬ PARTS USED: The aboveground part of the plant is used as medicine. The main ingredients of lady's mantle are tannins and flavonoids.

▬ MEDICINAL EFFECTS: The tannins prevent growth of certain bacteria, fight diarrhea and are a time-tested remedy for flaccid skin. The flavonoids invigorate the uterus and help with tension pains.

▬ APPLICATIONS: Lady's mantle tea is good for diarrhea. When consumed regularly, it has a cleansing effect on the skin and fights leucorrhoea ("the whites"). When consumed prior to the expected date of menses, the tea can help with menstrual pains. Lady's mantle tea is said to help with migraines and tension headaches. Regular sitz baths with infusions from lady's mantle are said to help with the inconveniences of leucorrhoea.

TEA:

Pour 1 cup boiling water over 2 teaspoons dried lady's mantle leaves, steep for ten minutes, then strain. Drink regularly as needed.

MIGRAINE TEA:

Mix 2 teaspoons dried lady's mantle leaves with 1 teaspoon dried mint leaves. Pour boiling water over the mixture; steep for ten minutes, then strain. Drink upon first onset of a migraine.

WOMEN'S ELIXIR:

Mix 1 teaspoon dried lady's mantle leaves, 1 teaspoon of dried marigold leaves and 1 tablespoon silverweed. Bring mixture to a boil with 2 cups milk; steep for 5 minutes, then strain. Season with honey and cinnamon. Alleviates menstrual pains.

SITZ BATH:

Boil 4 tablespoons dried lady's mantle leaves with 1 quart water; steep for ten minutes, then strain. Add decoction to sitz bath and bathe for ten minutes. Fights leucorrhoea.

IMPORTANT NOTE

People with a nervous stomach should test this herb with caution. Some patients report increased sensitivity.

Onion

Allium cepa

— SYNONYMS: Garden onion, edible onion

— PARTS USED: The bulbs of the onion are used as medicine. Onions contain primarily sulfuric compounds such as alliin, allicin, polysulfides and propanthial S-oxide. They are also rich in flavonoids and vitamin C.

— MEDICINAL EFFECTS: The sulfuric compounds have anti-inflammatory effects, stimulate the secretion of fluids and urination and facilitate healing. The flavonoids also have anti-inflammatory effects and vitamin C strengthens the immune system in general, thus indirectly also facilitating healing.

— APPLICATIONS: Onion can be used both internally and externally. Onion syrup or juice is recommended for colds and coughs, especially whooping cough. It has mucolytic and antitussic properties and soothes pharyngeal mucous membranes. Onion poultices or packs are recommended for earache, headache and swellings. Insect stings and corns can also be cured with onions.

DID YOU KNOW...

Onions also help corns: Sprinkle a little lemon juice on an onion slice and secure on corn using an adhesive bandage. Repeat daily for 1 to 2 weeks and the corn can then be easily peeled off.

Juice / syrup:

Peel and finely chop 1 onion. Cook with 1 cup water and 4 oz candy on a medium flame until syrupy; pass through a hair sieve and keep in a jam jar. Consume several teaspoons per day.

Milk:

Finely chop 2 onions in their peel. Bring to boil with 1 teaspoon honey, 1 clove, 1 thyme twig and a little water. Let rest for twelve hours, then pass through a fine sieve and boil with 1 cup milk. Drink 2 to 3 glasses per day.

Grated juice:

Peel onions and grate finely on an apple grater. Rub on swellings or insect bites. Rubbing the affected area with a freshly-cut onion also reduces swelling and itchiness.

Compresses / packs:

Peel and finely chop 1 onion, wrap in gauze cloth and place on aching ear (or on back of neck for headaches). Secure with a cap or scarf. Repeat several times.

Important note

Keep onion juice or onion pieces away from the eyes to avoid irritation.

Garlic

Allium sativum

▬ SYNONYMS: stinking rose

PARTS USED: The compound bulb of the garlic is used. Its main active ingredients are alllicin, saponin, vitamins, and selenium.

▬ MEDICINAL EFFECTS: Allicin and saponin have antibacterial and antimycotic effects. They dilate blood vessels and prevent the clotting of thrombocytes, thus preventing blood from clotting too fast. They are also said to lower cholesterol levels.

▬ APPLICATIONS: Drinking garlic juice affects intestinal fermentation processes and stimulates secretion of bile. It thus relaxes cramps and is said to support digestion. Consuming 3 to 5 cloves per day on a regular basis is said to have an anti-hypertensive effect, as the garlic dilates the blood vessels. Garlic fights inflammations and mashed garlic helps with warts, herpes and fungi.

IMPORTANT NOTE

Although garlic has no medical side effects, there is still 1 minor flaw: many people consider garlic's permeating smell unpleasant. The jury is still out on whether odor-free garlic preparations are as effective as those of fresh garlic.

JUICE:

Peel and mince 5 garlic cloves. Pulverize in a mortar with 5 teaspoons sugar. Add approximately 1 cup water and boil once, then steep for 5 minutes and filter through a cloth. Take by the spoonful.

OIL:

Peel and mince 4 garlic cloves. Grind in a mortar with 6 tablespoons olive oil. Apply oil to hardened muscles and massage thoroughly.

PASTE FOR WARTS AND HERPES:

Peel and mince 4 garlic cloves. Grind in a mortar with 2 to 3 tablespoons vinegar. Prepare the paste fresh daily and apply to warts or herpes. Remove after fifteen minutes.

VAGINAL SUPPOSITORY FOR CANDIDA ALBICANS (VAGINAL YEAST INFECTIONS):

Peel 1 garlic clove and slightly cut pulp. Wrap in a piece of gauze and firmly attach to a long piece of string. Insert clove into vagina and let act overnight; remove in morning. Repeat 3 to 4 times.

Ramson

Allium ursinum

■ SYNONYMS: bear's garlic, wood garlic, wild garlic

■ PARTS USED: The young leaves and roots are used. Only freshly collected leaves contain active substances, whereas the root can be stored and can be used similarly to Spanish onions. Ramson contains mainly essential oils, flavonoids, and vitamin C. The leaves contain folic acid, a group B vitamin.

■ MEDICINAL EFFECTS: In combination with the other active ingredients, the essential oils stimulate appetite and gastrointestinal functions. Folic acid has hemopoietic effects and enhances cell growth and vitamin C generally strengthens the body's defenses. States of enervation can be caused by a lack of these vitamins.

IMPORTANT NOTE

If you plan on collecting ramson yourself, be careful not to mistake leaves of lily of the valley for it, as the former are highly toxic. The correct herb, ramson, will give off a distinct odor reminiscent of garlic.

■ APPLICATIONS: Season food with the juice of ramson or with its finely chopped leaves or roots. This increases appetite, stimulates gastrointestinal functions and boosts the immune system. Ramson is also said to help against spring sluggishness.

Juice:

Put leaves in a juice extractor. You may want to thicken with buttermilk or kefir to make shakes. Your local market may offer ramson leaves in spring.

Pesto:

Chop 1 bunch of ramson leaves very finely. Prepare a paste from the chopped leaves, adding oil, salt and parmesan (if desired). Stored in a well-sealed, screw-top jar, this pesto can stay fresh for several weeks. It goes well with bread, pasta, potatoes or rice.

Galangal

Alpinia officinarum

■ SYNONYM: China root

PARTS USED: The galangal's rhizome is used. Active ingredients are galangol, essential oils, flavon derivatives and eugenol.

■ MEDICINAL EFFECTS: The active ingredients of galangal help with insufficient bile production, gastric juice secretion and poor appetite.

■ APPLICATIONS: Galangal tea stimulates production of bile and gastric juice and thus increases appetite. A paste made from galangal root is said to help with cardiac problems.

DID YOU KNOW ...

Galangal is also a condiment. It tastes similar to ginger and stimulates the digestion of fatty meals and heavy food. Galangal is also an ingredient in the popular medicinal digestive "Schwedenbitter."

TEA:

Pour 1 cup boiling water over 1 teaspoon dried, cut galangal root; steep for approximately 5 minutes, then strain. Drink 2 to 3 cups over the course of the day.

HONEY:

Mix 1 teaspoon galangal powder, 1 teaspoon marjoram powder and 1 teaspoon celery seed powder. Heat ½ lb honey in a water bath and stir in mixture. Take half a teaspoon 3 times daily over a period of 4 to six weeks. Instead of dried galangal, you can also use 2 tablespoons freshly chopped galangal.

IMPORTANT NOTE

Galangal induces menses and can cause premature menstruation or miscarriage.

Marshmallow
Althaea officinalis

▬ SYNONYMS: white mallow

▬ PARTS USED: The root, young flowers and leaves are used. The root contains mainly mucilage; the leaves and flowers contain essential oils and somewhat smaller amounts of mucilage.

▬ MEDICINAL EFFECTS: Mucilage has soothing effects in cases of inflammation of the mucous membranes, the airways or the gastrointestinal tract. It also softens hardened tissue associated with boils.

▬ APPLICATIONS: Marshmallow root tea is recommended for gastrointestinal problems and diarrhea. Gargling marshmallow root tea facilitates the healing of gingivitis as well as inflammations in the mouth and throat. Tea can also be made from the flowers and leaves, which, when sweetened with honey, can soothe a chronic cough. For boils, a hot pack with marshmallow paste is recommended. This promotes maturation of the boil and encourages a speedy remedy.

ROOT TEA:

Pour 1 cup cold water over 1 teaspoon dried, chopped marshmallow root. Steep for 30 minutes, stirring occasionally. Strain. Heat to drinking temperature (do not boil). Consume in small sips. Cold or lukewarm tea can be used for gargle.

TEA FROM LEAVES AND FLOWERS:

Pour 1 cup boiling water over 1 teaspoon dried, chopped marshmallow flowers and leaves. Steep for ten minutes, then strain. To drink for coughs, sweeten with honey or pear syrup.

POULTICES:

Immerse gauze in root tea (or make paste and spread on gauze: pour 1 cup cold water over 5 tablespoons dried, chopped marshmallow root. Let swell for 30 minutes, heat while stirring and spread on bandage). Place poultice on skin and, if necessary, wrap in a thick towel to retain heat.

TIP

For whooping cough and chronic bronchitis in infants, prepare marshmallow root as concentrate twice per day and drizzle 1 teaspoon onto a sugar cube. Administer 3 to 5 cubes per day. The tea can be kept in a sterile jar in the fridge for no longer than 3 days.

Dill

Anethum graveolens

▬ SYNONYMS: dill weed, garden dill

▬ PARTS USED: Usually the small, dark, oval seeds are used. The dried seed's main ingredients are essential oils, mineral substances and bitters.

▬ MEDICINAL EFFECTS: The essential oils of dill reduce flatulence, alleviate intestinal cramps, stomachache and abdomen conditions of women, as well as curing hiccups. Women in childbed may use dill to support lactation.

▬ APPLICATIONS: Drinking dill tea or dill wine before, during or after meals is said to prevent and alleviate indigestion. Hiccups can be alleviated by chewing dill seeds. Nursing women with lactation insufficiencies should, on a regular basis, drink dill tea or special nursing teas containing dill, anise, fennel and caraway. A sitz bath (hip bath) is recommended for abdominal conditions.

GARDENING TIP

The leaves also contain the fruit's active ingredients (although in a lower concentration) and can be used for remedial purposes.

TEA:

Grind 1 teaspoon dill seeds in a mortar. Pour over 1 cup hot water and steep for approximately ten minutes, then strain.

WINE:

Grind ten teaspoons dill seeds in a mortar. Bring to boil with 1 cup water and 1 cup white wine. Steep for 5 to ten minutes, then strain. Drink as punch or cold over the course of the day, with meals.

SITZ BATH:

Add 1 ounce seeds to 1 quart scalding hot water, cook briefly, then allow steep for fifteen minutes. Add to bath-water.

Angelica

Angelica archangelica

▬ SYNONYMS: garden angelica

▬ PARTS USED: Only the root is used. Minced and dried angelica root contains quantities of essential oils, bitters, tanning agents, furocoumarins, resins, wax and pectin.

▬ MEDICINAL EFFECTS: The essential oils interact with the bitters to increase appetite and act as a digestive aid and anti-convulsant. The secretion of bile is also stimulated. Angelica is said to act as an antitussic agent and can also be applied externally in cases of rheumatism.

▬ APPLICATIONS: When ingested regularly in tea form prior to meals, angelica is said to increase appetite. Tea from angelica can alleviate abdominal pains and cramps. Sipping angelica tea is said to reduce coughing fits and bathing in angelica or applying creams and ointments containing it as an active ingredient is said to relieve rheumatic pain.

IMPORTANT NOTE

The furocoumarins contained in angelica increase the skin's sun sensitivity and may, in combination with exposure to UV radiation, cause dermatitis. During the use of preparations containing angelica, therefore, it is recommendable to avoid extensive exposure to the sun.

Tea:

Boil 1 tablespoon finely chopped, dried angelica root in 1 cup water. Steep for 2 to 3 minutes, then strain. Drink 3 cups over the course of the day.

Wine:

Mix 2 oz finely chopped, dried angelica root with 1 quart white wine. Steep for approximately 5 to seven days, then strain. Store in a well-sealed bottle. Drink 1 port-wine glass in response to digestive ailments.

Baths:

For a full bath, boil approximately 4 oz dried and chopped angelica root in 1 quart water for approximately 15 minutes, then strain and add to hot bathwater. Rheumatics are recommended to take 2 15-minute angelica baths per week.

Celery

Apium graveolens

■ SYNONYMS: smallage, wild celery

■ PARTS USED: The stems, leaves, seeds and roots are used as medicine. The main active ingredients are essential oils, flavonoids, furanocumarins, vitamins and mineral substances.

■ MEDICINAL EFFECTS: The essential oils have a diuretic effect. The combination of flavonoids, vitamins, and mineral substances support healing, strengthen the immune system, contribute to energy metabolism and facilitate the recovery process in general.

TIP

Celery has been repeatedly recommended as a potency enhancer, though experts believe these claims are over-rated.

■ APPLICATIONS: The root is used to make juice, vegetable dishes or salads. All such preparations are diuretic and are thus recommended for kidney stones and kidney ailments in general. The tea from the dried leaves or from the seeds is also diuretic, and is additionally said to help with nervous weakness, inflammations of upper airways and chronic lung problems.

TEA:

In a pan, pour 1 cup cold water over 2 teaspoons celery leaves or crushed celery seeds. Boil, then strain. Drink lukewarm, in small sips and sweetened with honey, to cure chronic lung problems.

CELERY JUICE:

Brush and rinse a celery root and squeeze in a juice extractor. Consume 3 to 4 tablespoons per day: freshly-made celery juice has a high vitamin content. Store the freshly-made juice in the fridge. To add variety, mix the juice with other vegetable juices such as tomato juice or carrot juice.

Horseradish

Armoracia rusticana

SYNONYMS: red cole

PARTS USED: The root, which has main active ingredients mustard oil and glycosides gluconasturtiin and sinigrin, is used. The root is also rich in vitamin C and potassium.

MEDICINAL EFFECTS: The glycosides have an anti-bacterial effect; the mustard oil increases blood circulation in mucous membranes; vitamin C invigorates the body's defenses; and potassium stimulates the kidneys.

USES: Grated horseradish is recommended for infections of the urinary tract collection system and kidneys and for cases of bronchitis. Coughs and thick layers of mucus covering upper airways can be treated with a horseradish and honey mixture. Horseradish can also be applied externally: a horseradish pack is recommended for asthma, rheumatism, headaches, toothache or chronic tennis elbow.

DECOCTION:

Mix 1 tablespoon of freshly grated horseradish with 5 teaspoons honey and boil in 5 tablespoons water; remove quickly from burner. Consume 5 teaspoons over the course of the day.

SYRUP:

Mix 1 tablespoon freshly grated horseradish, 1 tablespoon finely chopped onion and 5 teaspoons honey; boil in 5 tablespoons water; remove quickly from burner. Cool. Consume 1 tablespoon 3 times per day.

PASTE FOR INTERNAL USE:

Mix equal parts of freshly grated horseradish and honey. Consume 1 tablespoon per day.

PASTE FOR EXTERNAL USE:

Mix 3 tablespoons freshly grated horseradish with 4 tablespoons low-fat curd cheese; apply ⅓ in layer to aching joints. Rinse off after ten minutes.

POULTICES:

Brush and rinse horseradish, grate root and spread a thin layer (about as thick as the back of a knife) onto a linen cloth. Place cloth on aching joints.

IMPORTANT NOTE

Excess consumption of horseradish can severely irritate mucous membranes and skin. Avoid contact of freshly grated horseradish with eyes: the hellish burn is very unpleasant!

Arnica

Arnica montana

■ SYNONYMS: mountain tobacco, leopard's bane

PARTS USED: Only the egg yolk-colored flowers are used. The main active ingredients contained in dried flowers are bitters, including sesquiterpene lactones, flavonoids and essential oils.

■ MEDICINAL EFFECTS: Arnica's essential oils have disinfectant and anti-inflammatory effects and stimulate healing. The flavonoids are thought to invigorate the cardiovascular system, especially in the elderly.

■ APPLICATIONS: Arnica is primarily applied externally. Used as a tincture or in bandages, it alleviates pain and relaxes muscles in cases of bruises, sprains or aching muscles and joints. It is also useful for the treatment of insect bites. As a gargle preparation, it has anti-inflammatory effects in cases of stomatitis and pharyngitis.

IMPORTANT NOTE

Ingestion of arnica is known to lead to severe poisoning. Therefore, it is not recommended for young children or elderly persons to gargle with arnica tea. Also, other arnica preparations may cause allergic reactions upon contact with sensitive skins.

Gargle preparation:

Pour 1 cup boiling water over 1 teaspoon arnica. Steep for ten minutes and strain. Allow to cool until lukewarm. Gargle twice per day until inflammation of the mucous membranes has receded.

Tinctures:

Pour 2 cups pure alcohol (ethanol, available in drugstores) over 2 oz arnica flowers. Steep for approximately ten days in a darkened place; strain and squeeze out residue. Dilute 1 teaspoon tincture with 2 cups water. Immerse gauze bandages in mixture until wet and place for ten minutes on blunt injury. Repeat 3 to 5 times per day.

Wormwood

Artemisia absinthium

SYNONYMS: none

PARTS USED: The whole herb, including the flower, is used. The main active ingredients are bitters such as absinthium, tannins and essential oils such as thujone, thujol and phellandrene. Wormwood is also used to flavor the drink absinthe.

MEDICINAL EFFECTS: The bitter absinthium stimulates not only bile secretion, but also that of other digestive fluids. The essential oils likewise improve the flow of digestive fluids. Thujone, thujol and phellandrene are all neurotoxins, which in large doses can cause spasms and severely degenerate the central nervous system. In small amounts, however, they have tranquilizing, soporific and balancing effects.

APPLICATIONS: Wormwood tea is a bitter-tasting tonic that helps with poor appetite and ailments of the gallbladder, stomach and intestines. The herb is especially helpful with gallbladder ailments such as gallstones, blocked secretion of bile or chronic biliary inflammations. The tea can reduce pain associated with severe menstrual disorders. Wormwood tea is recommended for rheumatism and colds. Applied externally, the tea improves complexion.

TEA:

Pour 1 cup boiling water over 1 teaspoon wormwood. Steep for approximately ten minutes, then strain. If suffering from poor appetite, drink 1 cup before meals; if suffering from ailments of the gastrointestinal tract or the gallbladder, drink 1 cup after meals. However, do not consume more than 2 to 3 cups per day. Drinking 1 cup daily serves as a preventative. Scrub skin with a cotton ball drenched in wormwood tea.

TEA MIXTURE:

Mix 1 teaspoon wormwood with 1 teaspoon peppermint. Add 1 cup boiling water. Steep for ten minutes, then strain. Drink 2 to 3 cups per day. The peppermint counters the bitterness of the wormwood.

TEA MIXTURE FOR GASTRIC PROBLEMS:

Crush in a mortar 1 teaspoon wormwood, half a teaspoon of gentian root, half teaspoon centaury, ½ in cinnamon stick and ½ teaspoon sour orange peel. Add 1 cup boiling water. Steep for ten minutes, then strain. Drink in small sips after meals.

IMPORTANT NOTE

Pregnant women and patients with liver complaints should avoid wormwood. Even a healthy individual should not drink more than 3 cups per day. Moreover, we generally advise against the consumption of wormwood tea over a period of more than 4 weeks, as it can cause damage to the central nervous system.

Mugwort

Artemisia vulgaris

■ SYNONYMS: felon herb, chrysanthemum weed, sailor's tobacco

■ PARTS USED: While the herb is in bloom, the tips of the shoots are gathered for use. The main active ingredients are bitters and the essential oils camphor and thujone.

■ MEDICINAL EFFECTS: The two essential oils act as an antiseptic and fungicide. Mugwort has digestive effects in that it increases secretion of the stomach, intestines and gallbladder. This herb is also said to be effective in fighting halitosis (bad breath) and nausea.

IMPORTANT NOTE

Do not drink mugwort tea during pregnancy – its consumption heightens the risk of miscarriage.

■ APPLICATIONS: Mugwort tea does not taste as bitter as wormwood, which is appreciated by most people. It helps in cases of indigestion and facilitates the production of bile - especially desirable after consuming fatty foods.

TEA:

Pour 1 cup hot water over 1 teaspoon mugwort sprouts. Steep for approximately 1 to 2 minutes, then strain. If needed, drink 1 to 3 cups over the course of the day.

WINE:

Make a preparation of 2 oz mugwort and 1 quart dry white wine. Have 1 glass before meals.

Asparagus
Asparagus officinalis

SYNONYMS: none

PARTS USED: The roots and shoots are used in medicine. The main active ingredients are asparagin, arginin, asparogosides, saponins, flavonoids and potassium.

MEDICINAL EFFECTS: The active ingredients stimulate the kidneys, aiding the passing of water.

APPLICATIONS: Asparagus root tea is recommended for mild incontinence, edema, bladder and kidney problems, and to prevent kidney stones. The tea is also popular for curing gout and rheumatism, since it facilitates excretion of waste products in urine. For poor complexion, dabbing the skin with a cold asparagus root decoction is recommended. Asparagus stalks - more of a vegetable than a medicinal plant today - have a very low calorie count and are diuretic. They rid the body of waste products and purify the blood. This is one reason why asparagus is the most popular vegetable for a spring detox. However, do not attempt an asparagus diet longer than ten days.

IMPORTANT NOTE

In extremely rare cases, excessive consumption of asparagus and asparagus root tea can lead to allergic skin reactions.

TEA:

Bring 1 teaspoon dried, pulverized asparagus root to a boil with 1 cup cold water, then strain. Drink 2 to 3 cups daily. The residual water from cooking asparagus stalks is also good to drink.

DECOCTION:

Boil 1 teaspoon dried, pulverized asparagus root with 1 teaspoon sea salt and 1 cup cold water, then strain. Cool and use to scrub skin.

ASPARAGUS REGIMEN:

Consume a daily portion of ½ lb asparagus over a 10-day period. Prepare the asparagus as follows: peel the stalks and simmer gently for 20 minutes in generously salted water, with a pinch of sugar and 1 pat of butter. Drink the cooking water as well. It is important not to consume asparagus along with fatty sauces, additional butter or other calorie-rich foods because the purifying effect will then be diminished.

Oats

Avena sativa

■ SYNONYMS: wild oats

PARTS USED: The grains without glumes are used as dietetic food and the young (green) oat straw is used as medicine. The active ingredients of oat grains are a large proportion of essential amino acids, group B vitamins, vitamin E, ferric iron, zinc and manganese. Oat straw primarily contains zinc, silicic acid and avenin.

■ MEDICINAL EFFECTS: Avenin has tranquilizing properties. Silicic acid and zinc facilitate healing of wounds. The amino acids, vitamins and trace elements in oat grains invigorate the weakened organism without overburdening the gastrointestinal tract.

■ APPLICATIONS: Oatmeal gruel is recommended for an upset stomach or as energy food during recovery from fits of weakness. The fibers of rolled oats and oat bran are said to bind cholesterol in the intestines and thus reduce the blood cholesterol level. Regular consumption of oat bran regulates bowel movements. Oat straw tea is recommended for insomnia, nervousness and increased levels of uric acid. A bath in a decoction of oat straw or in oat bran is said to help with itchiness, psoriasis and leg ulcers.

IMPORTANT NOTE

In excess doses, oat straw tea can cause headaches.

Oatmeal gruel / porridge / milk:

Boil 3 tablespoons rolled oats with 2 cups water or milk. Sweeten if desired.

Babies over the age of six months or infants with eating disorders or malnutrition may be pepped up effectively by mixing 1 tablespoon porridge oats into their milk.

Tea:

Pour 1 cup boiling water over 2 teaspoons fine oat straw. Steep for approximately ten minutes, then strain. Drink before going to bed.

Baths:

Simmer 2 handfuls fine oat straw in 3 quarts water for approximately 20 minutes, then strain. Add decoction to bathwater and bathe for approximately fifteen minutes. In addition, you may want to strew oat bran into the bathwater.

Poultices:

Simmer 1 handful fine oat straw in 1 quart water for approximately 20 minutes, then strain. Drench a linen cloth with decoction and wrap around slow-healing (but not open) wound.

Barberry
Berberis vulgaris

■ SYNONYMS: berbery, pipperidge bush

PARTS USED: The bright red fruit and its leaves are used. The fruit are rich in vitamin C, alpha hydroxide acid (AHA), mineral substances and trace elements. The leaves contain alkaloids.

■ MEDICINAL EFFECTS: The vitamin C in the barberry's red fruit invigorates the body's immune system. The active substances of barberry are also said to relieve morning sickness and lack of appetite. The alkaloids in the leaves are said to strengthen the heart.

■ APPLICATIONS: Barberry jelly or juice should be a regular component of your breakfast if you are hoping to increase your appetite or prevent morning sickness. Cardiotonic tea can be prepared from the leaves, but should be consumed only under medical supervision due the broad range of possible heart conditions; moreover, excess doses of the leaves can be toxic.

IMPORTANT NOTE

Only when ripe is the fruit free of harmful alkaloids. While unripe, the plant contains alkaloids and is mildly toxic. Excess dosages may lead to nausea, diarrhea, nosebleeds, kidney irritation and drowsiness.

TEA:

Pour 1 cup boiling water over 1 teaspoon dried barberry leaves. Steep for no longer than 5 minutes, then strain. 1 to 2 cups are permissible, but make sure to consult your doctor before treating ailments with barberry tea.

JUICE:

Boil 1 lb ripe fruit with ½ cup water until tender. Sieve. Dilute the paste with ½ quart to 1 quart water or apple juice. Sweeten with sugar or honey and pour into a sterile, sealable bottle. Store in the refrigerator and consume as soon as possible.

JELLY:

Boil 1 lb ripe fruit with ½ cup water until tender. Sieve. Boil the paste down to marmalade with an equal amount of sugar, adding other fruits such as berries or plums if desired.

Birch

Betula pendula

■ Synonyms: white birch

Parts used: Birch leaves, bark, resin and sap are used. The active ingredients in the leaves are primarily flavonoids, as well as essential oils, bitters, tannins, saponins and vitamin C. The sap contains agents for vegetal growth, organic acids and salts. The bark contains betulin, also known as birch camphor. The resin is rich in phenols and creosol and guaiacol in particular.

■ Medicinal effects: The leaves, which are the part most often used for medicinal purposes, have a strong diuretic effect without overworking the kidneys and are specially recommended for bacterial urinary tract infections and urethritis. They also have mildly anticonvulsant and disinfectant powers. In spite of the current lack of evidence from medical science, many people believe birch leaves to be the medicine of choice for rheumatism and gout.

■ Applications: Birch-leaf tea is a favorite for blood cleansing regimens in spring, as it flushes kidneys free of salts, grit and stones. The tea is also used for rheumatism. It is said that rubbing birch sap regularly into the scalp promotes hair growth and that washing with birch leaf helps improve complexion.

Important note

People who suffer from heart or kidney problems should avoid drinking birch-leaf tea. In such conditions, the adverse effects outweigh the desired reduction of edema.

TEA:

Pour 1 cup boiling water over 1 teaspoon dried birch leaves. Steep for ten minutes, then strain. Drink 1 quart over the course of the day, between meals. Drink water afterwards.

BLOOD CLEANSING REGIMEN:

Prepare a mixture from 3 oz birch leaves, 2 oz crushed fennel seeds, 2 oz balm leaves, 1 oz rosehip fruit, 1 oz elder flowers and 1 oz viola.

Pour 1 cup hot water over 1 teaspoon tea mixture. Steep for ten minutes, then strain. Drink 3 cups daily over 4 to six weeks to purify the body.

BATHS:

Pour 1 quart water over 3 to 4 handfuls birch leaves; boil and simmer at low temperature for ten minutes. Strain and add liquid to a full bath.

BIRCH LEAVES AS A SALAD INGREDIENT:

In spring, try adding a few fresh, young birch leaves to your lettuce.

Borage

Borago officinalis

■ SYNONYMS: burrage

■ PARTS USED: The whole herb in flower (except the root) and its seeds are used. Borage contains essential oils, silicic acid and, when fresh, lots of vitamin C. The seeds are rich in gamma linolenic acid.

■ MEDICINAL EFFECTS: The essential oils are said to influence the release of hormones and stimulate the nervous system. Gamma linolenic acid may alleviate skin diseases. The oil is used especially for neurodermatitis. Silicic acid contains silicon, which contributes to the growth of connective tissue, hair and nails.

■ APPLICATIONS: Borage oil is a recommended liniment for dry and irritated skin. People with neurodermatitis often suffer from enzyme problems, i.e. their bodies cannot produce gamma linolenic acid. Regular application provides them with this agent. Regarding internal use, borage in milkshakes or salads influences the adrenal glands and thus alleviates melancholia and nervousness. Regular consumption of borage is also recommendable for those who suffer from brittle nails or hair because silicic acid has a positive influence on the firmness of hair and nails. Borage flowers and wort must not be applied over a longer period of time, however, due to certain alkaloids suspected of having carcinogenic properties.

Borage & buttermilk shake:

Mix 5 tablespoons finely chopped borage with 2 cups buttermilk. Season with salt, pepper and a splash of green Tabasco sauce. You may want to garnish the shake with blue borage flowers.

Poultices:

Pour 1 cup boiling water over 4 tablespoons finely chopped borage. Steep for ten minutes, then strain. Immerse a linen or gauze cloth until wet and place on inflammation. Repeat several times per day.

Borage oil:

Rub affected parts with borage oil 2 to 3 times per day. Available in health food stores.

Mustard

Brassica nigra, Sinapis alba

▬ SYNONYMS: none

▬ PARTS USED: The seeds of the plant are medicinal. The main active ingredient is the glycoside sinigrin, which, when combined with water, breaks down into allyl isothiocyanate and glucose. Furthermore, the seeds contain mucilage, other essential oils and fatty acids.

▬ MEDICINAL EFFECTS: The allyl isothiocyanate (mustard oil) stimulates blood circulation, revitalizes and purifies skin and has an antibiotic effect. Mustard oil increases blood circulation in mucous membranes, the vitamin C strengthens the immune defense and potassium stimulates the kidneys.

▬ APPLICATIONS: Mustard is primarily used externally. Mustard poultices are administered in the treatment of rheumatic ailments, pleuritis and bronchitis. A footbath with mustard flour stimulates blood circulation and thus helps alleviate certain forms of headache. Used internally, mustard increases appetite. Many people attribute their longevity, or the fact that they have not had a cold in years, to eating one teaspoon of spicy mustard a day. It is a proven fact that eating mustard increases circulation in the throat, which in turn stimulates (and therefore strengthens) the body's defenses.

MUSTARD USED AS MEDICINE:

Eat 1 teaspoon household mustard every day before lunch.

POULTICES:

Make a paste from 4 oz mustard powder and water. Spread on gauze or linen cloth and place for 5 to ten minutes on affected area. For children, do not leave a mustard pack on chest for longer than 5 minutes. Afterwards, wash affected area thoroughly and apply lotion.

FOOTBATH:

Fill a small tub with lukewarm water and stir in 2 to 4 tablespoons mustard flour. Bathe feet in mixture for 5 minutes, rinse with lukewarm water, dry and apply lotion.

IMPORTANT NOTE

Excessive use of mustard can badly irritate mucous membranes or skin. Avoid contact with eyes - mustard burns considerably.

Cabbage

Brassica oleracea

▬ SYNONYMS: European cabbage, white cabbage

▬ PARTS USED: The cabbage leaves, which contain active ingredients vitamin C, group B vitamins, mineral substances, bitters and mustard oil glycosides are used. In addition, white cabbage contains the so-called anti-ulcer factor (also known as "vitamin U"), discovered in 1950.

▬ MEDICINAL EFFECTS: As its name suggests, the anti-ulcer factor helps prevent gastric ulcers. The bitters, mustard oil glycosides and vitamin C all have positive effects on mucous membranes and skin.

▬ APPLICATIONS: Drinking freshly squeezed cabbage juice helps with gastric and duodenal ulcers. This regimen involves the consumption of one quart cabbage juice per day over 4 to six weeks, accompanied by a light diet. Cabbage leaves are used externally as wrappings for leg ulcers, herpes zoster, inflammations of the nail bed and the breast, light burns and rashes. Inhaling cabbage vapors is said to get rid of headaches.

> **DID YOU KNOW ...**
>
> Aside from white cabbage, there are other cabbage species that are good for your health and have an anti-ulcer factor.

JUICE:

Squeeze the leaves of 1 cabbage using juice extractor. You will need about 4 lbs cabbage for 1 quart juice. The juice must be prepared fresh daily; better still, twice a day.

POULTICES:

Blanch inner leaves of cabbage, allow to drip and cut out midrib. Roll with rolling pin until tender, then place on affected area. Fix with a gauze bandage and replace twice a day.

VAPOR BATH:

Finely grate quarter cabbage. Boil for fifteen minutes. Place contents in a dish and inhale hot vapor for approximately ten minutes, with a towel over the head.

Marigold
Calendula officinalis

■ SYNONYMS: calendula, holibud, summer's pride

■ PARTS USED: The marigold flowers are used. Their famous active ingredient is calendula sapogenin, but the flowers also contain saponins, glycosides, essential oils, carotenoids, xanthophyls, bitters and mucilage.

■ MEDICINAL EFFECTS: Calendula sapogenin has anti-inflammatory effects. Saponins are said to reduce the blood fat level and inhibit growth of melanomas. The essential oils have an anti-microbial effect, especially against fungi and bacteria. Carotenoids and xanthophyls strengthen the body's defenses.

■ APPLICATIONS: Marigold flowers are mainly used externally. Calendula ointment is used for chronic wounds, nail bed infections and leg ulcers; poultices are used for sprains and dislocations, abscesses, contusions and burns. Used internally as tea, marigold is recommended for gallbladder ailments, light gastric cramps and menstrual pains. Their pleasing color makes marigold flowers a popular ingredient in many tea mixtures. Gargling with marigold tea is recommended for inflammations of mucous membranes in the mouth.

TIP

Breastfeeding often causes inflammations of the nipple. Regular application of calendula ointment keeps nipples soft and supple.

Tea:

Pour 1 cup boiling water over 1 teaspoon marigold flowers; strain after ten minutes. Drink 3 cups over the course of the day. Use cold as a gargle.

Calendula milk:

Mix 1 teaspoon marigold leaves with 1 teaspoon silverweed and 1 teaspoon lady's mantle leaves. Heat with 1 cup milk; steep for 5 minutes, then strain. Sweeten with honey and add cinnamon if desired. This milk is very effective for menstrual pains.

Calendula butter / calendula ointment:

Crush 2 handfuls fresh marigold flowers. Along with 2 oz butter, steep in hot water, stirring constantly, for twenty minutes. Pass through gauze and cool. Place in sterile container and keep in the fridge. Remove from fridge approximately half hour prior to application.

Poultices:

Pour 1 cup boiling water over 2 tablespoons flowers and steep for ten minutes. Immerse a linen cloth in infusion and wrap around injury. Cover with a towel and let act until cloth is cold. Repeat several times per day.

Shepherd's purse
Capsella bursa pastoris

■ SYNONYMS: blindweed, witches' pouches

■ PARTS USED: The aboveground part of the plant is used. The active ingredients of shepherd's purse are flavonoids, potassium and a peptide with haemostatic effects.

■ MEDICINAL EFFECTS: The flavonoids strengthen the uterus, the haemostatic peptide alleviates heavy menstrual flow and nosebleeds and potassium regulates the body's water balance.

■ APPLICATIONS: Shepherd's purse tea is recommended for heavy menstrual flows. A cotton swab soaked in the tea can stop nosebleeds. The herb is an ingredient of many teas that purify the blood and is said to have a tonifying impact on the heart. This can be explained by the herb's high potassium content: the heart is a muscle and, as such, needs potassium for its contractions.

TIP

Young, finely chopped shepherd's purse is a popular ingredient in spring salads. If collecting the herb yourself, avoid areas frequented by dogs or near main roads.

Tea:

Pour 1 cup boiling water over 2 teaspoons dried shepherd's purse. Steep for approximately ten minutes, then strain. Consume 2 cups per day during menstruation.

Nose insert:

Pour 1 cup boiling water over 2 tablespoons dried shepherd's purse. Steep for approximately ten minutes, then strain. Soak a cotton swab with lukewarm solution and insert into affected nostril. Remove after approximately fifteen minutes.

Caraway

Carum carvi

▬ SYNONYMS: wild cumin, Roman cumin, Persian cumin

▬ PARTS USED: The seeds of caraway are used. Their main active ingredients are essential oils, the most important being carvon, which comprises 60% of the seeds' essential oils.

▬ MEDICINAL EFFECTS: Carvon acts primarily on the gastrointestinal tract. It stimulates production of gastric juice, and soothes and relaxes the intestines. The growth of useful microorganisms is facilitated while the proliferation of harmful bacteria is blocked.

▬ APPLICATIONS: Drinking caraway tea with your meals facilitates digestion and prevents flatulence and bloating. Seasoning heavy food with caraway also increases production of digestive fluids, making these meals more digestible. The application of caraway pouches has proven useful in treating baby colic. In a similar fashion to anise and fennel, caraway stimulates lactation and is thus recommended to nursing mothers and women in childbed. Chewing on caraway seeds fights bad breath.

TEA:

Pour 1 cup boiling water over 2 teaspoons crushed caraway seeds; steep for approximately fifteen minutes, then strain. Drink 1 cup before meals.

CARAWAY POUCHES:

Put caraway seeds in a small linen pouch. Heat pouch in water. Place warm pouch on baby's tummy several times a day for a few minutes. Replace seeds at least once per week.

IMPORTANT NOTE

Please do not attempt to collect caraway seeds yourself. Caraway is easily confused with other umbelliferae, such as wild chervil, and some of these plants are mildly toxic.

Chestnut

Castanea sativa

▬ SYNONYMS: European chestnut, sweet chestnut

▬ PARTS USED: The longish, lancet-shaped leaves, which contain tannins and flavonoids when dried, are used. The chestnuts themselves are good to eat.

▬ MEDICINAL EFFECTS: The leaves are used as medicine for conditions of the upper respiratory system, whooping cough, asthma and pharyngitis. However, current medical science provides no evidence to this effect.

▬ APPLICATIONS: A tea is made from dried leaves, of which, two to 3 cups a day should successfully treat bronchitis, whooping cough or asthma. Cold tea is used for gargling in cases of pharyngitis.

TEA:

Pour 1 cup cold water over 1 teaspoon dried, chopped chestnut. Boil briefly, straining after 3 minutes. As needed, drink 2 to 3 cups per day. Use cold or lukewarm several times per day as a gargle.

IMPORTANT NOTE

Do not confuse European chestnut with horse chestnut, which is also a household remedy. Horse chestnut has different ingredients and effects; also of the latter, the chestnuts themselves are used.

Centaury

Centaurium erythraea

▬ SYNONYMS: centaury gentian, feverwort

▬ PARTS USED: The aboveground part of the plant is used. Its main active ingredients are the bitters amarogentin and gentiopicrin. Furthermore, the herb contains flavonoids and sterols.

▬ MEDICINAL EFFECTS: Amarogentin and gentiopicrin stimulate secretion of digestive fluids.

▬ APPLICATIONS: Centaury tea can be used to counter poor appetite, insufficient production of gastric juices, flatulence and to prevent gallstones. Those with strongly hyperacidic stomachs should avoid centaury. The active ingredients of the plant stimulate blood circulation and help fight nervous exhaustion. Centaury is also said to alleviate migraine headaches.

> IMPORTANT NOTE
>
> While an overdose of centaury is highly unlikely and the herb has no known side effects, we do not recommend its use for those suffering from gastric ulcers or enteritis.

TEA:

Pour 1 cup cold water over 1 teaspoon dried centaury; steep for six to ten hours, then strain. Heat and drink decoction. Sweeten with honey.

TEA MIXTURE:

Mix 1 teaspoon dried centaury with 1 teaspoon fennel and 1 teaspoon peppermint. Pour 1 cup boiling water over the mixture; steep for ten minutes, then strain. Drink 2 to 3 cups over the course of the day. This tea has a more agreeable taste.

Greater Celandine

Chelidonium majus

■ SYNONYMS: garden celandine, tetterwort

■ PARTS USED: The root and weed are used as medicine. The main active ingredients are various alkaloids, which are similar to opium alkaloids. Aside from these, the plant contains saponins, flavonoids and essential oils.

■ MEDICINAL EFFECTS: The alkaloids have relaxing and anticonvulsant effects on the gastrointestinal tract. A cytotoxic alkaloid helps to cure warts.

APPLICATIONS:

A celandine tea regimen of 3 to 4 weeks supposedly helps with ailments of the stomach, intestines and gallbladder. It is crucial to use fresh herbs, since their healing ability deteriorates fast. The fresh sap is popular for its positive results when applied to warts.

IMPORTANT NOTE

Large doses of celandine are toxic. Hypertonic persons should avoid internal use of celandine.

TEA:

Pour 1 cup boiling water over 1 teaspoon dried celandine. Steep for approximately ten minutes, then strain. Drink 3 to 4 cups per day, over the course of 3 to 4 weeks. Drops of celandine tincture are more effective because the proportion of active ingredients in the weed varies greatly. Shortly after half a year, the active ingredients have evaporated and the leaves are useless.

Chicory

Cichorium intybus

■ SYNONYMS: succory, French endive, Italian dandelion

■ PARTS USED: The herb as a whole, including flower and root, is used. The main active ingredients are tannins and bitters.

■ MEDICINAL EFFECTS: The tannins starve out harmful bacteria in mucous membranes and the bitters stimulate secretion of digestive fluids.

■ APPLICATIONS: Chicory tea is a bitter-tasting tonic that increases appetite, mobilizes the liver and stimulates the flow of bile. Chicory tea cures bloating, flatulence and diffuses abdominal pains. Used externally, chicory is said to help with skin disorders.

TIP

You can easily collect and dry chicory – the herb is ubiquitously found on waysides, embankments, and untilled land. It is easily distinguished from other species. Make sure, though, not to collect chicory near popular dog-walking spots. Bundled in sheaves, you can dry chicory in a dark place or in the attic.

Tea:

Pour 1 cup cold water over 1 teaspoon dried chicory root or herb. Boil. Simmer for approximately 2 to 3 minutes. Strain and drink 2 to 3 cups over the course of the day. Sweeten with honey if desired.

Tea mixture:

Mix 1 teaspoon dried chicory root or leaf with 1 teaspoon of peppermint. Pour 1 cup cold water over the mixture and boil. Simmer for approximately 2 to 3 minutes. Strain and drink 2 to 3 cups over the course of the day. Sweeten with honey if desired.

Cleansing tonic:

Pour 2 cups cold water over 4 tablespoons dried chicory root or leaf, and boil. Simmer for approximately to 3 minutes. Strain when cool. Drench a cotton ball with decoction and scrub skin.

Cinnamon

Cinnamomum zeylanicum

▬ SYNONYMS: Ceylon cinnamon

▬ PARTS USED: The bark of the cinnamon tree or cinnamon shrub is used. Cinnamon contains essential oils, mucilage and tannins, as well as eugenol, thymol and cumarin.

▬ MEDICINAL EFFECTS: The essential oils prevents growth of bacteria and fungi spores. Cinnamon stimulates bowel movements and increases production of gastric juice.

▬ APPLICATIONS: Cinnamon tea can help with indigestion, lack of appetite, bloating and light crampy pains of the upper abdomen. Heavy menstruation recedes after drinking cinnamon tea. Gargling with cinnamon liqueur cures coughs and hoarseness. Cinnamon milk facilitates sleep during colds. Traditional medicine uses cinnamon oil for the healing of wounds. Because it stimulates blood circulation, cinnamon is said to alleviate pains associated with rheumatism. Migraine patients can massage their temples with a little cinnamon oil to soothe pain.

IMPORTANT NOTE

Pregnant women or patients suffering from gastrointestinal ulcers should not use cinnamon internally in any form, be it tea, liqueur or oil.

TEA:

Crush 2 small morsels of cinnamon stick and submerge in 2 cups boiling water; steep for ten minutes under a lid, then strain. Drink 1 cup before and 1 after meals.

MILK:

Stir equal small pinches of ground cinnamon, ground cardamom, ginger powder and clove powder into 1 glass hot milk.

LIQUEUR:

Crush 2 cinnamon sticks and fifteen cloves in a mortar. Grind ¼ teaspoon nutmeg and finely chop several peppermint leaves. Place together in a wine bottle and top up with sherry. Cork bottle, steep for ten days, then strain. Drink 1 liqueur glass full before or after meals. Gargle with liqueur to fight coughs or hoarseness.

OIL:

Crush 3 to 4 cinnamon sticks in a mortar and submerge in half a cup of neutral edible oil. Steep for approximately ten days, then strain and pour into a small bottle. Cinnamon oil is also available at pharmacies, well-assorted drugstores and natural food stores.

Lemon

Citrus limon

━━ SYNONYMS: none

━━ PARTS USED: The fruit of the lemon tree are used. The main active ingredients are vitamin C, flavonglycosides and essential oils.

━━ MEDICINAL EFFECTS: Vitamin C invigorates the body's defenses, the essential oils stimulate appetite and digestion and the flavonglycosides have a slightly antibacterial effect.

━━ APPLICATIONS: Hot lemon juice is the remedy of choice for imminent colds and influenza infections. Even if a cold is well underway, the mucolytic quality of lemon juice causes inflammation to recede. Citric acid and vitamin C are also successfully used externally in treatment of warts or swellings after insect bites.

TIP

Store lemons in the vegetable compartment of your fridge so that they stay fresh as long as possible. There will always be an opportunity to put lemons to good use.

Hot sweet lemon:

Squeeze juice from 2 lemons. Heat same amount of water and combine with lemon juice. Sweeten with sugar or honey. Sip while juice is as hot as possible. Remain in bed afterwards.

Lemon slices:

Quickly putting a lemon slice on an insect sting can prevent swelling and itchiness.

Lemon juice plaster:

Douse a cotton ball with freshly squeezed lemon juice. Place on wart and secure with an adhesive bandage. Replace twice per day. Observe routine over two to four weeks. This therapy has made many a wart disappear.

Footbath:

If suffering from sweaty or smelly feet, add 1 tablespoon lemon juice to bathwater and bathe daily.

Coriander

Coriandrum sativum

■ SYNONYMS: Chinese parsley

■ PARTS USED: The fruit of coriander are used. The active ingredients are essential oils and tannins.

■ MEDICINAL EFFECTS: The essential oils and tannins have an anticonvulsant effect, prevent the growth of bacteria and facilitate digestion.

■ APPLICATIONS: Coriander tea helps stimulate appetite and relieve indigestion. Combined with fennel and caraway, coriander is especially effective for gastrointestinal cramps.

TIP

Coriander is present in many curry mixtures. It is a condiment which also makes heavy food more digestible.

TEA:

Grind 1 teaspoon coriander in a mortar. Pour 1 cup boiling water over ground coriander, steep for approximately ten minutes, then strain. Drink 1 cup coriander tea before meals.

TEA MIXTURE:

Crush in a mortar 1 teaspoon coriander with 1 teaspoon caraway and 1 teaspoon fennel. Pour 1 cup boiling water over the mixture, steep for approximately ten minutes, then strain. Drink 3 to 4 cups over the course of the day.

Hawthorn

Crataegus oxyacantha

■ SYNONYMS: whitethorn, quickthorn

■ PARTS USED: The flowers, leaves, and berries of hawthorn are used as medicine. Their main active ingredients are procyanidins, followed by flavonoids, biogenic amines and potassium.

■ MEDICINAL EFFECTS: The combination of active ingredients increases blood circulation in the myocardial muscle, stabilizes heart rate and increases activity of myocardic cells.

■ APPLICATIONS: Hawthorn tea, often used for various cardiovascular problems, should be consumed during a regimen lasting at least 4 weeks. Both homemade and ready-made hawthorn preparations are recommended treatments for an aging heart, degenerations of the myocardial muscle, sclerotic changes of the coronary vessels and poor circulation. Likewise, the tea is recommended for circulatory insufficiency, hypertension and age-related insomnia.

IMPORTANT NOTE

A recurring rumor claims that hawthorn tea helps lose weight. The truth is that the tea is mildly diuretic, so the scales will budge a bit in your favor; however, no body fat is actually metabolized.

TEA:

Pour 1 cup boiling water over 1 teaspoon dried hawthorn leaves and flowers. Steep for fifteen minutes, then strain. Drink 2 to 3 cups over the course of the day.

TEA MIXTURE TO STRENGTHEN THE HEART:

Mix 1 teaspoon dried hawthorn leaves and flowers with 1 teaspoon arnica flowers and ½ teaspoon balm. Pour 1 cup boiling water over the mixture. Steep for ten minutes, then strain. Drink 2 cups per day.

TEA MIXTURE FOR INCREASED BLOOD CIRCULATION:

Mix 1 teaspoon dried hawthorn leaves, 1 teaspoon dried yarrow and 1 teaspoon peppermint. Pour 1 cup boiling water over the mixture. Steep for ten minutes, then strain. Drink 3 cups per day.

Oilseed pumpkin

Cucurbita pepo

SYNONYMS:
field pumpkin, squash

PARTS USED:
The seeds of oilseed pumpkin are used. Their main active ingredients are phytosteroles, vitamin E, selenium, essential oils and fatty oils.

TIP

You may make pumpkin seeds a regular component of your diet by adding small amounts to various dishes, baking your own pumpkin seed bread, or sprinkling roasted pumpkin seeds over ice-cream and other desserts.

MEDICINAL EFFECTS:
The phytosteroles are thought to have a positive effect on the tonus deficiency associated with benign prostate gland tumors and irritable bladder.

APPLICATIONS: A pumpkin seed regimen is recommended for an irritable bladder or the early stages of benign prostate gland tumors. Bedwetting is also said to be curable with pumpkin seed (unless organic causes for enuresis are present). Pumpkin seed oil and pumpkin seeds are said to drive out tapeworms if administered in the right dosage.

REGIMEN FOR MALADIES OF THE URINARY TRACT:

Coarsely chop 2 to 3 tablespoons pumpkin seeds with a knife and consume on an empty stomach in mornings as well as before lunch and dinner. Wash down with a glass of water. This regimen ought be observed for 3 to 4 months and pumpkin seeds ought be eaten regularly before breakfast thereafter. The seeds need not be chopped, but must be chewed thoroughly.

TAPEWORM REGIMEN:

Swallow 3 to 6 tablespoons macerated pumpkin seed oil in 1 gulp. Maintain regimen for 2 weeks. Pumpkin seed oil is very tasty, but if your stomach cannot handle its oiliness, you may want to try the alternative of eating 1 handful pumpkin seeds and washing them down with a glass of milk. The resulting soft, diarrhea-like feces is part of the desired effect.

Carrot

Daucus carota

■ SYNONYMS: wild carrot

IMPORTANT NOTE

Earlier theories claiming that harm results from an excess consumption of, or even intoxication with, provitamin A are possibly incorrect. More recent research shows that vitamins contained in natural food have stronger potential effects than vitamin supplements present in popular vitamin drinks or effervescent tablets.

Parts used: The root is used. The active ingredients are primarily provitamin A (better known as carotene), and vitamins B1, B2 and C. Furthermore, carrots contain flavonoids, essential oils and carotatoxin.

■ MEDICINAL EFFECTS: The combination of vitamins contained in carrots facilitates healing, strengthens the immune system, contributes to energy metabolism, supports recovery and maintains general good health.

■ APPLICATIONS: The carrot's ingredients have the most effect when consumed raw. The more finely chopped the root, the better the absorption of active ingredients. From these two facts follows that the best effect is reached with freshly made carrot juice. Furthermore, one ought to add a few drops of oil (or eat something containing fats along with the carrot juice) since it facilitates the absorption of the lipophilic provitamin A. Carrot paste is also recommended for infants being weaned because it supports digestion and prevents constipation and flatulence.

CARROT JUICE:

Brush and rinse carrots, then squeeze in juice extractor. Stir in 3 to 4 drops quality vegetable oil (wheat germ oil or rapeseed oil) per glass. Best consumed when fresh as vitamin content is highest. If storing carrot juice in the fridge, add some lemon juice to prevent juice turning brown.

MIX DRINKS:

Apples, pineapple or oranges make tasty mixed drinks with carrot juice.

CARROT PASTE FOR BABIES:

Brush, rinse and finely chop 2 to 4 carrots. Cook until tender with 1 cup water for fifteen to 20 minutes, then make a paste in blender. Do not salt or season. If spoon-feeding the paste, mix in ¼ teaspoon wheat germ oil. Alternatively, mix 2 to 3 tablespoons paste with ready-made nursing milk in feeding bottle. Well-sealed leftovers can be kept for a day in the fridge, but paste should then be cooked briefly. While cooking the paste destroys vitamins. It also kills possible germs.

Cardamom

Elettaria cardamomum

■ SYNONYMS: bastard cardamom, grains of paradise

■ PARTS USED: Cardamom seeds, which have essential oils as their main active ingredient, are used.

■ MEDICINAL EFFECTS: The essential oils stimulate production of gastric juice and facilitate bowel movements. The also have an anticonvulsant effect.

■ APPLICATIONS: Drinking cardamom tea is said to support digestion. It helps against flatulence and is also said to alleviate stomach pains and cramps. Chewing the seeds or gargling with cold cardamom tea freshens breath and helps with chronic bad breath. Folklore has it that cardamom tea also cures hangovers.

TIP

Cardamom may be mixed with black tea and consumed in portions over the course of the day.

TEA:

Pour 1 cup boiling water over 1 teaspoon crushed cardamom seeds. Steep for approximately ten minutes, then strain. Drink 1 cup before meals.

SPICED APPLE JUICE:

Crush together in a mortar 1 teaspoon cardamom seeds, 1 teaspoon coriander seeds, 1 teaspoon caraway and ½ teaspoon star-anise seeds. Add 1 teaspoon balm and boil in 1 quart apple juice. Allow to cool, then strain. Sweeten with honey and pour into a sterile bottle. Keep in the fridge; drink 1 liqueur glass per day.

Field Horsetail

Equisetum arvense

▬ SYNONYMS: shave-grass, scouring rush, Dutch rushes

▬ PARTS USED: Only the bare stem is used. Minced and dried horsetail is rich in flavonoids and mineral nutrients and contains large quantities of silicic acid and potassium salt.

▬ MEDICINAL EFFECTS: In combination with its potassium and silicic acid, the flavonoids of horsetail are diuretic. Silicic acid contains large amounts of silicon, an essential trace element for the human body. In particular, fast-growing tissue such as mucous membranes, skin, hair and nails consume a lot of silicon, though the silicon contained in silicic acid also facilitates healing. Furthermore, silicon enhances the skin's propensity to bind moisture and supports the growth of connective tissue and the healthy development of hair and nails. As an organism gets older, however, it retains less silicon, which reduces the elasticity and tension force of binding tissue and its ability to retain water.

▬ APPLICATIONS: If ingested regularly in tea form, field horsetail can cure urinary tract infections and edemas of the legs, due to its diuretic effect. Horsetail tea is also recommended for gout, since it helps flush out toxins. Gargling with or mouth rinsing with horsetail tea facilitates the healing of gingivitis and pharyngitis and washing wounds with a horsetail decoction or applying a wet pack facilitates the healing of chronic or slow-healing wounds.

IMPORTANT NOTE

Regular consumption of horsetail tea is not recommendable for persons with heart or kidney problems.

TEA:

Boil 1 tablespoon dried field horsetail with 1 cup water for 5 minutes. Steep for ten to fifteen minutes, then strain. Drink 3 cups over the course of the day. Because the tea can taste quite bitter, it is advisable to wash down with a glass of water.

BATHS:

For a full bath, add 3 handfuls field horsetail to bathwater. Soak in bath for approximately ten minutes.

Poultices:

Boil 1 quart water with 6 tablespoons dried herbs. Simmer for roughly half an hour, then strain. Immerse sterile, absorbent gauze in the decoction. Apply. Change bandage 2 to 3 times per day.

Buckwheat

Fagopyrum esculentum

■ SYNONYMS: brank, beechwheat, Indian wheat

■ PARTS USED: The herb and seeds of buckwheat are used. The root contains mainly rutic acid (rutin) and other flavonoids and tannins. The seeds are rich in protein and group B vitamins.

■ MEDICINAL EFFECTS:
Rutin is said to fight circulatory disorders, vein insufficiencies, varices and edema. It increases the permeability of blood in the capillaries. B vitamins contribute to energy level, metabolism and strengthening the nervous system.

■ APPLICATIONS: A regular use of buckwheat tea for two to 3 weeks may have a positive impact on blood vessels. Buckwheat tea is said to promote quality sleep, though the seeds are usually processed and used as flour or grits for cooking and baking. Buckwheat porridge is considered an energy diet for the convalescent.

Tea:

Add 1 teaspoon buckwheat herb to 1 cup boiling water and cook for approximately 1 minute. Steep for ten to fifteen minutes, then strain. Drink 2 to 3 cups over the course of the day.

Tea mixture:

Pour 1 cup boiling water over 1 teaspoon buckwheat herb, 1 teaspoon currant leaves and 1 teaspoon mistletoe. Steep for ten to fifteen minutes, then strain.

Porridge:

Boil 4 tablespoons buckwheat grits with 1 cup water. Cook for approximately 1 minute. Sweeten with honey. This porridge can also be prepared with milk.

Did you know ...

Buckwheat is not related to wheat. The buckwheat family is part of the Polygonales order.

Meadowsweet

Filipendula ulmaria

SYNONYMS: bridewort, lady of the meadow, meadow queen

PARTS USED: The flowers (and occasionally the whole plant) are used as medicine. The active ingredients are flavonoids, tannins and salicylic acid compounds.

IMPORTANT NOTE

Avoid meadowsweet tea during pregnancy as it can trigger labor.

MEDICINAL EFFECTS: The flavonoids are sudorific and lower body temperature. The salicylic acid compounds have an anti-inflammatory effect.

APPLICATIONS: Meadowsweet tea is primarily used in combination with other medicinal plants to treat colds. It is also recommended for the bladder and kidneys and as a remedy for gout. Meadowsweet reduces cramps and alleviates pain associated with tension headaches.

Tea mixture for headaches:

Mix 2 teaspoons meadowsweet with 1 teaspoon viola, 2 teaspoons St. John's wort and 1 teaspoon clover. Pour 2 cups boiling water over the mixture. Steep for approximately fifteen minutes, then strain.

Tea mixture for gout:

Mix 2 teaspoons meadowsweet with 1 teaspoon lovage root, 1 teaspoon birch leaves and 2 teaspoons nettle leaves. Pour 1 quart boiling water over the mixture. Steep for approximately fifteen minutes, then strain. Drink 1 quart per day over the course of 3 weeks. Wait 2 weeks before repeating regimen.

Fennel

Foeniculum vulgare

■ SYNONYMS: sweet fennel, wild fennel

■ PARTS USED: Fennel seeds are used as medicine. The active ingredients are essential oils; among them, sweet trans-Anethole and fenchone (which has a taste reminiscent of camphor) are crucial.

■ MEDICINAL EFFECTS: The essential oils promote expectoration of mucous bronchial tubes, work as a carminative (thus stimulating the appetite), help alleviate flatulence and stimulate lactation in nursing mothers.

■ APPLICATIONS: Fennel tea can be given even to breast-feeding babies and the tea is also highly recommended for children and adults. This tea can be used as an expectorant for whooping cough, bronchitis and other infections of the upper airways. It also helps with flatulence and prevents breastfeeding babies from vomiting. As it has anticonvulsant effects in both the upper and lower abdomen, it may be worth trying this tea in treatment of menstrual pains. Nursing women with breast milk insufficiencies can increase lactation by drinking fennel tea regularly.

TIP

Fennel can also be prepared as a vegetable.

Tea:

Pour 1 cup boiling water over crushed seeds. Steep for approximately ten minutes, then strain. For colds, sweeten with honey. Administer 3 to 5 teaspoons of unsweetened fennel tea to sucklings prior to nursing.

Milk:

Boil 1 cup milk. Pour boiled milk over crushed seeds. Steep for ten minutes, then sieve. Sweeten with honey as desired.

Syrup:

Crush 3 teaspoons fennel seeds in a mortar, cook with half pint water for approximately 5 minutes, then strain. Cook with 4 oz cane sugar until syrupy. For coughs or bronchitis, consume six tablespoons per day.

Wine:

Crush 2 teaspoons fennel seeds with 2 teaspoons horehound and 1 teaspoon coneflower. Boil 1 teaspoon mixture with 1 cup white wine. Steep for 3 to 5 minutes, then strain. Sweeten with honey as desired and drink while still hot, then rest in bed for at least 1 hour. Helps with bronchitis.

Strawberry

Fragaria vesca

▬ SYNONYMS: wood strawberry

▬ PARTS USED: Usually the leaves, fruit and, occasionally, the roots of the plant are used. The main active ingredient in the leaves and roots are tannins. The fruit are rich in vitamin C.

▬ MEDICINAL EFFECTS: The tannins are said to help treat gastrointestinal trouble, diarrhea and inflammations of the mucous membranes. The vitamin C invigorates the body's defenses.

▬ APPLICATIONS: Strawberry tea is recommended for mild gastric trouble and diarrhea. Drinking or gargling with the tea has an analgesic effect in cases of stomatitis or pharyngitis. A daily portion of strawberries in summer invigorates the body's defenses.

IMPORTANT NOTE

Certain individuals may respond with eczema to the consumption or external use of strawberries. Cultivated strawberries contain large amounts of vitamin C, but do not collect and dry strawberry leaves if chemical fertilizers or herbicides have been used. Strictly speaking, only the wood (or wild) strawberry is considered a medicinal plant.

Tea:

Pour 1 cup boiling water over 1 teaspoon dried, chopped strawberry leaves. Steep fifteen minutes, then strain. Drink in small sips or gargle with lukewarm tea. Repeat three times per day. If using strawberry root in the tea's preparation, half the amount of powdered root is sufficient.

Facial tonic/mask:

Simply mash fresh strawberries and apply juice to skin, e.g. after sunburn. A soothing mask made from strawberries, a little cream and honey will smooth dry, hardened skin.

Ash

Fraxinus excelsior

▬ SYNONYMS: common ash, European ash, weeping ash

▬ PARTS USED: The slim, lancet-like leaves (with the midrib removed) are used as medicine. The active ingredients of the leaves are mainly rutin and other flavonoids, bitters, tannins, cumarins and essential oils.

▬ MEDICINAL EFFECTS: Ash leaves have a mildly diuretic effect.

▬ APPLICATIONS: Ash tea stimulates the kidneys without causing irritation. The subsequent increased kidney function ensures that waste products such as uric acid are excreted. For this reason, ash tea is recommended for gout and rheumatism. The tea is said to cleanse the blood and can also be used as mild laxative.

TIP

Ash leaves are easy to collect. Let them fade a bit before crushing them lightly with a rolling pin. Sprinkle water on the leaves and dry in a dishcloth, suspended in a warm place.

TEA:

Boil 1 teaspoon dried ash leaves with 1 cup water. Simmer for three minutes, then strain. Drink 2 cups ash tea per day for at least fourteen days for rheumatism and gout.

Fumitory
Fumaria officinalis

■ SYNONYMS: earth's smoke, beggary, vapor

■ PARTS USED: The above-ground part of the plant is used. Its main active ingredients are fumaric acid and bitters.

■ MEDICINAL EFFECTS: Fumaric acid regulates bile secretion and skin metabolism, which is why this herb is also recommended for psoriasis. The bitters are diuretic and are said to help with constipation.

■ APPLICATIONS: Fumitory tea regulates bile secretion and helps flush out small gallstones. Itchiness, scabies and psoriasis (insofar as they respond to fumarin therapy) can be soothed by drinking fumitory tea as well. Difficulty in passing water or bowel movements, which is likely to be associated with cramps, can be remedied by drinking fumitory tea.

IMPORTANT NOTE

Do not drink more than three cups of fumitory tea per day. Excessive consumption of fumitory can cause stomachache.

Tea:

Pour 1 cup boiling water over 1 teaspoon dried, chopped fumitory. Steep for ten minutes, then strain. Sweeten with honey or pear syrup, as the tea tastes bitter. Alternatively, let the tea cool and prepare a non-alcoholic spritzer using apple juice or another type of sweet fruit juice.

Tea mixture for skin conditions:

Mix ½ teaspoon of dried, chopped fumitory with half teaspoon marigold flower. Pour 1 cup boiling water over the mixture, steep for ten minutes, then strain. This tea is not as bitter as the pure fumitory tea mentioned above, but has similar effects.

Tea mixture for internal ailments:

Mix equal parts fumitory, birch, nettle and balm. Pour 1 cup boiling water over 1 teaspoon tea mixture, steep for ten minutes. Strain. This tea mixture is quite pleasant in taste and therefore facilitates regular consumption.

Gentian
Gentiana lutea

■ SYNONYMS: yellow gentian, bitterwort, pale gentian

■ PARTS USED: The root of the yellow gentian is used. The main active ingredients are bitters (especially gentiopikrin), tannins and essential oils.

■ MEDICINAL EFFECTS: The bitters serve as a tonic for the stomach and are generally prescribed for medical conditions related to the stomach, intestines, liver or gallbladder.

■ APPLICATIONS: Gentian tea stimulates production of bile and gastric juice and thus increases the appetite. It prevents flatulence and has a positive effect on the mucous membranes in the mouth. The tea boosts circulation. In combination with other herbs, yellow gentian is also said to cure gastric neurosis.

TEA:

Pour 1 cup boiling water over 1 teaspoon dried and chopped yellow gentian root. Steep for five minutes, then strain. Drink before meals. Caution: this tea tastes very bitter!

TEA MIXTURE:

Pour 2 cups boiling water over ½ teaspoon dried and chopped yellow gentian root, ½ teaspoon crumbled cinnamon stick, 1 teaspoon sour orange skin and ½ teaspoon centaury. Steep for five minutes, then strain.

TINCTURES:

Steep 2 oz gentian root for one week in 2 fluid oz of 60% alcohol; filter before drinking. Consume 1 tablespoon with half glass of water to treat lack of appetite or insufficient digestion. Take 20 drops mixed with sugar for overall invigoration.

Licorice

Glycyrrhiza glabra

▬ SYNONYMS: none

▬ PARTS USED: The root is used. Its main active ingredients are flavonoids, especially liquiritin and liquiritigenin, as well as glycyrrhizin and sterols.

▬

MEDICINAL EFFECTS: The glycyrrhizin blocks inflammations and protects mucous membranes. The flavonoids have an anticonvulsant effect.

▬ APPLICATIONS: Licorice tea or syrup with licorice powder is recommended for curing coughs, bronchitis and stomach ailments such as gastritis.

IMPORTANT NOTE

Excessive consumption over several weeks can lead to hypertension and edema.

TEA:

Pour 1 cup boiling water over 2 teaspoons chopped licorice root. Steep for ten to fifteen minutes under a lid, then strain. Drink 3 to 5 cups over the course the day.

TEA MIXTURE FOR GASTRITIS:

Mix 2 teaspoons chopped licorice root with 1 teaspoon chamomile and 1 teaspoon balm leaves. Pour 1 cup boiling water over the mixture. Steep for five to ten minutes, then strain. Drink 1 cup after meals.

WINE:

Place 2 oz chopped licorice root in a wine bottle and fill up with white wine. Cork the bottle and let rest for ten days. Filter through cloth. Add 1 tablespoon licorice wine to 1 glass water and use as gargle morning and evening. Fights excess mucus and bad breath.

Ivy

Hedera helix

▬ SYNONYMS: English ivy

▬ PARTS USED: The herb's leaves and spiked flowers are used as medicine. The dried leaves contain saponins and flavonoids.

▬ MEDICINAL EFFECTS: The saponins have anti-inflammatory, mucolytic and expectorant effects and serve as a fungicide when used externally. They tend to irritate skin and mucous membranes. The flavonoids are mucolytic and anticonvulsants.

▬ APPLICATIONS: Tea can be made from the dried leaves and one should drink no more than two cups per day in treatment of common cold and whooping coughs. Ivy schnapps is also said to be useful. Used in a footbath, ivy fights unpleasant athlete's foot. Massaging the scalp with an ivy decoction can prevent dandruff. Regular massages of problem areas with ivy oil are said to deal with insufficiency of connective tissue and with orange-peel skin.

IMPORTANT NOTE

Do not drink more than 2 cups ivy tea or more than 1 tablespoon ivy & violet spirit, as saponins in large amounts are toxic and can lead to unwanted irritations of mucous membranes and skin.

Tea:

Pour 1 cup boiling water over 1 teaspoon dried, chopped ivy leaves. Steep for ten minutes, then strain. Sweeten with honey.

Ivy & violet spirit (ivy schnapps):

Put 1 oz each coarsely chopped, fresh ivy leaves and coarsely chopped violet flowers in a sealable wine bottle and top up with gin or vodka. For four weeks, shake preparation daily, then strain and decant in a new bottle. Consume ½ teaspoon daily.

Infusion/Footbath:

Pour 1 quart boiling water over 2 tablespoons dried, chopped ivy leaves (or fresh, chopped ivy leaves). Allow to cool, strain. Massage infusion into scalp. A footbath can be made from 5 quarts water and 1 quart infusion. Bathe feet for ten to fifteen minutes.

Massage oil:

Chop one handful fresh ivy leaves and one rosemary twig coarsely, place in a screw-top jar and top up with half pint olive oil. Allow to rest in a warm place for two weeks, then strain. Thoroughly squeeze out residue. Pour massage oil into an opaque bottle and massage problem areas regularly.

Sunflower

Helianthus annuus

■ SYNONYMS: none

■ PARTS USED: The petals and seeds of the sunflower are used. The active ingredients in the petals are flavonglycosides, anthocyans, xanthophyll, sapogenin and solanthene acid. The seeds are especially rich in fatty oils and linoleic acid. It contains carotenoids, lecithin and lots of vitamin E.

■ MEDICINAL EFFECTS: The active ingredients in the flowers reduce fever and are even said to help with malaria. The oil from the kernels is used externally for scaly skin, chronic wounds, and aching joints.

■ APPLICATIONS: Drinking sunflower petal tea reduces fever. For malaria in particular, the tea is said to be a reliable anti-fever aid. The kernels produce an oil that can be used as body lotion for dry skin, for the healing of wounds and for soothing aching joints. The so-called oil extraction regimen originated in Siberia. Proponents of this regimen claim that it extracts toxic substances from the body which concentrate overnight in mucous membranes of the mouth. However, the success of this regimen has not been substantiated in any scientific study. In any case, regular oil extraction is a natural way to clean the teeth and has a whitening effect.

TEA:

Pour 1 cup boiling water over 2 teaspoons dried sunflower petals, steep for ten minutes, then strain. Sweeten with honey and drink 2 to 3 cups per day when feverish.

TEA MIXTURE:

Mix 2 teaspoons dried sunflower petals with 1 teaspoon lime flowers. Pour 1 cup of boiling water over the mixture, steep for ten minutes, then strain. Sweeten with honey and drink 2 to 3 cups per day when suffering from feverish colds.

SIBERIAN OIL EXTRACTION REGIMEN:

First thing in the morning, swish 1 tablespoon macerated sunflower oil in mouth for ten to fifteen minutes, sucking the oil hard through teeth. Spit out oil. You will know you did it correctly if the oil you spit out is white throughout. Brush teeth afterwards. It is important not to swallow the oil, but to spit it out.

DID YOU KNOW THAT ...

Polyunsaturated fatty acid can prevent cardiovascular diseases and have positive effects on cholesterol levels. As little as half an ounce of sunflower oil covers the recommended adult daily intake of vitamin E.

Sea buckthorn

Hippophae rhamnoides

■ SYNONYMS: sallowthorn

■ PARTS USED: The sea buckthorn fruits are used. The active ingredients are vitamin C, mineral substances, flavonoids and fatty oils in the seeds of the fruit.

■

MEDICINAL EFFECTS: The vitamin C boosts the body's defenses and improves healing - the body requires an additional supply of this vitamin during a fever. The flavonoids have anti-inflammatory and antibiotic effects. The oil is recommended for skin diseases.

■ APPLICATIONS: Sea buckthorn juice is recommended for the prevention and relief of colds. Sea buckthorn can be administered to children by the spoonful during the cold and flu season. Regular consumption of sea buckthorn jelly increases the body's defenses and can thus prevent colds. The oil is rich in essential fatty acids, vitamin E, beta-carotene and palmitoleic acid and is thus recommended for dry skin and dandruff. It protects against UV radiation and facilitates healing.

DID YOU KNOW ...

During seaside holidays in the fall, do not pluck buckthorn berries because it will bruise the ripe fruit too much. Instead, cut them off using scissors and let them drop into a cloth.

Syrup:

Rinse 1 lb sea buckthorn fruit, cut into halves, let swell overnight in 1 cup water. Boil the mixture briefly, and sieve. Sweeten with honey or pear syrup if desired. Pour syrup into sterile, sealable jars. Store in the fridge and consume 1 tablespoon per day.

Jelly:

Let 1 lb sea buckthorn fruit swell and cook in same manner as for the syrup (above). Bring fruit paste to boil with 1 cup sea buckthorn juice, the juice of 1 lemon and a 1½ lb jam sugar. Pour jelly into sterile jars and use daily as spread or stir into yogurt.

Hops

Humulus lupulus

SYNONYMS: none

PARTS USED: The cones of the female plant are used. The active ingredients are bitters, essential oils, flavonoids, tannins and polysaccharides.

MEDICINAL EFFECTS: The bitters lupulon and humulon have a soothing and tranquilizing effect. The essential oils, primarily methylbutenol, have a soothing effect on the central nervous system. The flavonoids, especially xanthohumol, are used by menopausal women and by men suffering from premature ejaculation. The so-called procyanidines, which belong to the group of tannins, dilate blood vessels. The polysaccharides help with menopausal ailments.

APPLICATIONS: Hop tea is a popular soporific. Hop tincture is even more effective but should only be used before going to sleep. Hop baths, hop pillows, or hop milk are also popular household remedies for sleeping disorders. Hop tea can be administered for treatment of hot flashes, compulsive sweating, and other menopausal ailments. Rubbing irritated or sensitive skin with hop facial tonic has a soothing effect.

TIP

Due to the fact that they cause drowsiness, hops should only be taken before going to bed. We strongly advise against focused work, operating machinery or driving after consuming hops.

TEA:

Pour 1 cup boiling water over 2 teaspoons dried hops. Steep for ten minutes, then strain. Sweeten with honey and drink before going to bed.

MILK:

Boil 1 cup milk with 2 teaspoons dried hops. Steep for five minutes, then strain and sweeten with honey.

BATH:

Place 2 handfuls hops cones in a linen pouch and suspend in bathwater. Bathe for no longer than ten minutes.

PILLOW:

Put 2 handfuls hops cones in a linen pouch and place in pillowcase. Replace cones every two weeks.

FACIAL TONIC:

Pour 1 cup boiling water over 2 teaspoons dried hops. Steep for ten minutes, then strain. Prepare a 3:1 solution with alcohol and pour into a sterile, opaque, sealable bottle. Twice per day, morning and evening, soak a cotton ball in tonic and rub on face.

St. John's wort

Hypericum perforatum

■ SYNONYMS: St. John's grass, Klamath weed

PARTS USED: The flowers and leaves of St. John's wort are used, and their active ingredients are essential oils, tannins, flavonoids and hypericin.

■ MEDICINAL EFFECTS: The essential oils have a tranquilizing effect and the flavonoids affect the cycle of serotonin levels. Serotonin is also known as the "happy hormone." A high serotonin level in the brain increases overall well-being and contentment. Serotonin assists in the alleviation of pain and helps with problems falling asleep. Hypericine blocks depression, ensures quality sleep and keeps you active during the day.

IMPORTANT NOTE

After regular consumption of St. John's wort, some people show an increased sensitivity to sunlight and develop a predisposition towards sunburn.

■ APPLICATIONS: Regular consumption of St. John's wort tea (or tea mixtures containing the herb) stimulates secretion of bile and regulates blood circulation. Consumed over a long period of time, the tea may alleviate depression. St. John's wort oil can be applied externally and used for rheumatism, sunburns and lumbago. It facilitates healing and alleviates pain associated with sprains, dislocations, hematomas and herpes zoster.

Tea:

Pour 1 cup boiling water over 2 teaspoons St. John's wort. Steep for ten minutes, then strain. Drink 3 to 4 cups over the course of the day. For treatment of depression, the tea may take up to four weeks of consumption to register effect.

Tea mixture for hypertension:

Mix 2 teaspoons St. John's wort with 1 teaspoon balm, 1 teaspoon arnica flowers, 1 teaspoon milk thistle seeds and 1 teaspoon speedwell. Pour a 2 cups boiling water over the mixture. Steep for approx. fifteen minutes, then strain and sweeten with honey. Drink in several portions over the course of the day.

Oil:

Grind 3 handfuls fresh flowers in a mortar. Pour along with 2 cups soy oil into a sealable jar and leave for six weeks in a sunny place. Shake daily. When the oil has turned red, pass through a cloth and squeeze out residue. Pour oil into a sealable bottle.

A wet pack with St. John's wort oil:

Place 1 egg yolk in a high tumbler and stir in 2 tablespoons St. John's wort oil, drop by drop. Let this emulsion act on inflamed skin for half an hour and rinse with lukewarm water.

Hyssop
Hyssopus officinalis

■ SYNONYMS: none

■ USED PARTS/CONSTITUENTS: The upper part of the flowering plant is used. Aside from essential oils and tannins, the main ingredient of hyssop is sitosterol.

■ MEDICINAL ACTION: The essential oils have anticonvulsant and mucolytic effects. The tannins help to kill bacteria and thus fight inflammations. Sitosterol stimulates the urinary tract and is said to have therapeutic value in treating benign prostate carcinomas.

■ USES: Hyssop tea is used primarily to treat gastrointestinal ailments, especially flatulence and lack of appetite. It has a slightly anticonvulsant and diuretic effect on the bladder. Gargling the tea also helps with dry coughs. In this country, hyssop is not particularly popular as a culinary herb. This is a shame, as it makes an excellent herbed cottage cheese, is a great condiment in stews, soups and salad, making dishes generally more digestible.

TIP

You can buy hyssop seed and sow the plant yourself because it is an extremely hardy perennial. Aside from being an effective medicinal plant and a useful culinary herb in the kitchen, the attractive hyssop makes a pretty addition to any flower garden.

TEA:

Pour 1 cup cold water over 2 teaspoons dried, chopped hyssop. Bring the mixture to boil, let steep for five minutes, then strain.

ANTICONVULSANT TEA MIXTURE:

Mix 1 teaspoon dried, chopped hyssop with ½ teaspoon thyme and ½ teaspoon St. John's wort. Pour 1 cup cold water over the mixture. Bring to boil, let steep for five minutes, then strain. Drink 2 cups daily, 1 before breakfast and 1 before going to sleep.

HERBAL CURD CHEESE:

Stir 4 tablespoons finely chopped hyssop into ½ lb cottage cheese, along with a little olive oil, salt and pepper. Eat this curd cheese along with baked potatoes or as a spread.

Walnut

Juglans regia

▬ SYNONYMS: stone-nut, common walnut

▬ PARTS USED: The longish, lancet-shaped leaves are used medicinally, as is the oil extracted from the delicious nuts. The dried leaves contain tannins, essential oils and flavonoids.

▬ MEDICINAL EFFECTS: The tannins starve out harmful bacteria in mucous membranes. The essential oils help with mycosis and the flavonoids have anti-inflammatory properties.

▬ APPLICATIONS: Walnut leaf tea is administered for irritated mucous membranes and can bring relief in cases of diarrhea induced by irritated intestinal lining. Stomatitis, gingivitis and inflammations in the eye area can be cured with walnut leaves. Applied externally, walnut leaves are said to help with acne, eczema and hemorrhoids. Walnut oil contains a fairly high amount of linolenic acid, which belongs to the group of essential fatty acids. It is said to help with rheumatic arthritis. Many patients have reported that regular consumption of products containing linolenic acid has brought relief and increased mobility to their aching joints.

TEA:

Pour 1 cup cold water over 2 teaspoons dried, cut walnut leaves. Boil briefly and strain after three to five minutes. Drink 2 to 3 cups per day when required. Use cool or luke-warm several times a day for gargling.

EYE RINSING:

Mix 1 teaspoon dried, cut walnut leaves with 1 tea-spoon of chamomile flowers. Pour 1 cup water over the mixture and boil briefly. Strain after three to five minutes. Cool.

POULTICES:

Pour 1 cup cold water over 2 teaspoons dried, cut wal-nut leaves. Boil briefly and strain after three to five minutes. Immerse a linen cloth (or a cotton ball) in the decoction. Place on eczema or rub skin with the cotton ball.

SITZ BATH:

Mix 2 tablespoons dried, cut walnut leaves with 2 tablespoons oak bark. Pour 2 cups cold water over the mixture, bring briefly to boil and strain after ten minutes. Then add to bathwater and bathe for ten to fifteen min-utes.

Juniper

Juniperus communis

■ SYNONYMS: none

■ PARTS USED: The ripe fruits are used, which are rich in essential oils, especially pinenes.

■ MEDICINAL EFFECTS: Pinenes have a strong diuretic effect and stimulate blood circulation in the bronchial tubes and intestines.

■ APPLICATIONS: Drinking juniper tea (or, alternatively, chewing up to ten juniper berries per day) is recommended as a regimen for preventing urinary stones as well as for gout and rheumatism. Chewing juniper berries can stop a coughing fit and increase the appetite. Unpleasant bloating after an unduly rich meal can also be fought by chewing a juniper berry. Juniper can also be used externally: a sitz bath is said to help with hemorrhoids. Rubbing inflamed or rheumatic joints with juniper oil or a tincture is said to bring relief.

IMPORTANT NOTE

Pregnant women and nephritis patients ought to avoid juniper. Do not exceed recommended consumption of juniper berries or use them over a period longer than six weeks because in high amounts the berries are suspected of harming the kidneys rather than aiding recovery.

TEA:

Crush 2 to 3 juniper berries in a mortar. Pour 1 cup boiling water over berries. Steep for no longer than five minutes, then strain. Drink 1 to 3 cups over a maximum period of six weeks.

TINCTURE:

Crush 1 oz dried juniper berries in a mortar. Top up with ½ cup brandy and steep for one week. Strain into an opaque, sterile flask. Splash some of the tincture on a gauze cloth and wrap around aching or rheumatic joints.

OIL:

Crush 1 oz dried juniper berries in a mortar. Pour half a cup of olive oil over the berries and steep for two weeks. Strain and pour into an opaque, sterile flask. Massage aching joints with the oil.

SITZ BATH:

Put ¼ teaspoon of juniper oil in warm bathwater, and bathe for ten minutes.

Deadnettle

Lamium album

■ SYNONYMS: white deadnettle

■ PARTS USED: The flowers of deadnettle are used. Their main active ingredients are saponins, mucilage, tannins and essential oils.

■ MEDICINAL EFFECTS: The effects of the saponins are anti-inflammatory and especially fungicidal. The tannins relieve cramps and the essential oils increase appetite.

■ APPLICATIONS: Deadnettle tea is said to help with irregular or painful menstruation and vaginal discharge. Sitz baths are also said to help against such discharge and an inflammation of the nailbeds can be cured with a handbath or footbath. Deadnettle tea is said to help with catarrhs of the upper airways and with minor occurrences of stomatitis and pharyngitis. Deadnettle tea also cures minor gastrointestinal ailments.

TIP

In spring, collect young deadnettles - their leaves can be prepared in similar ways to spinach.

Tea:

Pour 1 cup boiling water over 1 teaspoon dried deadnettle flowers; steep for ten minutes, then strain. Drink 3 to 4 cups over the course of the day for at least four weeks but not more than eight weeks.

Tea mixture for light vaginal discharge:

Mix 1 teaspoon dried deadnettle flowers with 1 teaspoon yarrow and 1 teaspoon lady's mantle. Pour 1 cup boiling water over the mixture; steep for ten minutes, then strain. Consume 2 to 3 cups over the course of the day for a period of two weeks.

Sitz bath, footbath, or hand-bath:

Pour 2 cups boiling water over one handful dried deadnettle flowers. Steep for at least half an hour, strain and add decoction to hot bath water.

Lavender

Lavandula angustifolia

■ SYNONYMS: lavendula, garden lavender, common lavender

■ PARTS USED: The lavender flowers, which contain as their main active ingredient the essential oil with its pleasant flagrance, are used. Furthermore, the flowers contain tannins, flavonoids, phytosterols, and cumarins.

■ MEDICINAL EFFECTS: The essential oil has a soothing effect on the central nervous system. The tannins are said to help with diarrhea and lavender is suitable for stimulating secretion of bile.

■

APPLICATIONS: Lavender tea can be used as a tranquilizer for nervousness, anxiety and sleeping disorders. It is sometimes recommended as an anticonvulsant or diuretic cure. A massage with lavender oil is said to alleviate rheumatic pains. A bath in lavender is simultaneously soothing and refreshing and is especially recommended for hypotonic patients. Sleeping in lavender flowers is said to cure sleeping disorders and facilitate a deep and refreshing sleep.

IMPORTANT NOTE

The commercially available small bottles of lavender oil contain a distillate from the flowers, a concentrated mixture of essential oil which may be applied only by small drops. If you want to use this oil for massaging, first mix 1 to 2 drops with 1 tablespoon edible oil.

TEA:

Pour 1 cup boiling water over 2 teaspoons lavender flower; steep for five to ten minutes, then strain. Sweeten with honey. Drink 2 cups, preferably before bedtime.

SOOTHING TEA MIXTURE FOR THE RESPIRATORY TRACT:

Mix 1 teaspoon lavender flower with 1 teaspoon peppermint. Pour 1 cup of boiling water over the mixture, steep for five to ten minutes, then strain. Sweeten with honey. Drink 3 cups per day.

OIL:

Strip 1 handful dried or fresh lavender flowers from stems, place in a screw-top jar and fill with 1 cup olive oil. Steep for 3 days in a sunny and warm place. Strain the oil, squeezing out flower residue. Store in an opaque bottle.

BATH:

Pour 1 quart boiling water over 4 oz flowers; steep for ten minutes, then add decoction to bathwater.

Lovage
Levisticum officinale

- **SYNONYMS:** Alexanders, black pot-herb

- **PARTS USED:** The root (and occasionally the herb as a whole) is used. Essential oils are the main active ingredient in both, but their concentration is higher in the root.

- **MEDICINAL EFFECTS:** The essential oils are diuretic and have a mildly anticonvulsant effect, also preventing bloating, heartburn and indigestion.

- **APPLICATIONS:** Lovage tea is recommended as a flushing therapy for inflammations of the urinary tract and for prevention of kidney stones. Lovage tea is also recommended for heartburn and indigestion. Lovage is often used in combination with other medicinal plants.

IMPORTANT NOTE

Pregnant woman should avoid lovage as its consumption can irritate the kidneys and cause nausea and dizziness.

TEA:

Pour 1 cup cold water over 1 teaspoon dried lovage root. Boil and strain immediately. Drink 2 cups per day.

TEA MIXTURE:

Mix 1 teaspoon dried lovage root, 1 tablespoon parsley fruit and 1 teaspoon rosehip seeds. Pour 1 cup cold water over the mixture and boil. Steep for several minutes. Strain. Drink 2 cups per day.

TIP

1 teaspoon dried lovage root will always improve a stock or broth. When the whole herb is used, it should always be cooked a short while to develop full effect.

Flax

Linum usitatissimum

▬ SYNONYMS: linseed

▬ PARTS USED: The flaxseed is used. The main active ingredient is mucilage in high concentrations, enhanced by the presence of fatty acids. Flaxseed contains a high amount of fiber and is rich in linolenic acid.

▬ MEDICINAL EFFECTS: The mucilage produces a protective layer over inflamed mucous membranes. Fiber stimulates bowel movements and the linolenic acid is said to help with rheumatism.

▬ APPLICATIONS: Flaxseed tea is a time-proven gargle for stomatitis, pharyngitis and gingivitis. It is also said to help with coughs, hoarseness and gastritis. Shredded flax, consumed from a spoon or mixed with granola, serves as an effective laxative because the seeds swell and their expansion in the large intestine stimulates bowel movements and the excretion of feces. Regular consumption of one to two tablespoons flaxseed oil in cold meals is said to reduce the inflammation of joints in rheumatic patients. Mush poultices with flaxseed soften ulcers and boils, facilitate the healing of eczema and are said to alleviate toothache when placed on the cheek.

IMPORTANT NOTE

Do not use when breastfeeding or give to constipated infants: flax seed contains traces of hydrogen cyanide.

TEA:

Pour 1 cup cold water over 1 to 2 tablespoons flaxseed – freshly shredded seeds are best. Allow to swell for 20 minutes; heat lightly and strain. Use for gargling or drink in small sips.

REGIMEN FOR CHRONIC CONSTIPATION:

Stir 2 to 3 tablespoons flaxseed into every meal – whole seeds are best when freshly shredded. Apply over a period of 3 months. Always wash down with a glass of water.

MUSH POULTICES:

Fill gauze or linen pouch with 3 to 6 tablespoons shredded flaxseed. Pour hot water over pouch and place on affected area; leave until cool.

FLAX OIL:

Flax oil can be manufactured at home only with difficulty; therefore, it is preferable to purchase it in small amounts, as macerated oil, from natural food stores. Because of its high linoleic acid content, flax oil has a short shelf life compared to other edible oils. Consume by regularly adding 1 to 2 tablespoons to cold dishes or salads.

Mallow

Malva sylvestris

▬ SYNONYMS: high mallow, common mallow, cheese flower

▬ PARTS USED: The flowers and leaves of mallow are used as medicine. The main ingredient is mucilage, besides which, mallow also contains essential oils and tannins.

▬ MEDICINAL EFFECTS: Mucilage reduces irritation and creates a protective layer. The essential oils have mucolytic and anticonvulsant effects.

▬ USES: Mallow tea alleviates stomatitis and pharyngitis and treats mild cases of diarrhea. Gargling is recommended for fighting coughs. Sore throats and hoarseness can be cured with this tea. Mallow can also be used externally, in combination with other medicinal plants, to alleviate inflammations and to serve as a tranquilizer.

TEA:

Pour 1 cup boiling water over 2 teaspoons dried mallow flowers or leaves and strain after fifteen minutes. When cold, this tea makes a good gargle.

HERB PILLOW:

Mix 4 tablespoons mallow flowers or leaves with 4 tablespoons mallow, 4 tablespoons yellow sweet clover and 4 tablespoons flax seed; place in linen pouch. Heat water and soak pouch for ten minutes. Place on inflamed areas of skin (such as boils) and secure with a towel. Leave on skin until pouch cools. Repeat several times per day.

TIP

The flower (flowers) of the mallow are said to be more effective than the leaves. The jury is still out on this issue, however, which is why most pharmacies stock mixtures as well as pure mallow flowers.

POULTICES:

Mix 5 tablespoons mallow flowers or leaves with 5 tablespoons chamomile flowers. Pour 1 cup boiling water over the mixture and steep for ten minutes. Immerse a linen cloth in decoction and place on eczema. Leave until cloth is cold. Repeat several times per day.

Chamomile

Matricaria recutita

▬ SYNONYMS: German chamomile, wild chamomile

▬ PARTS USED: The flower heads, because they are rich in essential oils such as chamazulene and bisabolene, are used. Other active ingredients include flavonoids, tannins and valerian acid.

▬ MEDICINAL EFFECTS: The essential oils of chamomile have anti-inflammatory effects. Chamomile is thus administered in cases of inflammatory ailments of the digestive tract and the respiratory tract. Chamomile is also used for skin disorders such as acne or abscesses, chronic wounds or inflammations of the nail bed.

▬ APPLICATIONS: When consumed regularly, chamomile tea helps with gastric disorders, sickness, nausea and enteritis. Gargling or rinsing the mouth with chamomile tea facilitates healing of gingivitis, stomatitis and pharyngitis. Chamomile vapors alleviate coughs and influenza infections. A chamomile bath is recommended for chronic wounds, hemorrhoids or inflammations of the nail bed.

TIP

Chamomile can be administered as early as infanthood. When a child is suffering from teething pains, you may want to put a small amount of chamomile oil on the baby's gums using your index finger.

TEA:

Pour 1 cup hot water over 1 tablespoon chamomile. Steep for ten minutes, then strain. Drink 3 to 4 cups over the course of the day.

BATHS:

Depending on type of bath desired, i.e. footbath, hand-bath, sitz bath or full bath, add between 2 tablespoons and 2 handfuls chamomile to bathwater. Bathe for approx. ten minutes.

INHALATION:

Place 3 tablespoons chamomile in a shallow dish. Add hot water and lower face over dish, covering head and back of neck with a bath towel. Inhale for ten minutes. Repeat twice per day during an influenza infection.

POULTICES:

Wrap chamomile in a gauze cloth; pour hot water over pouch and press it to inflamed skin for five minutes.

OIL:

Pulverize 1 handful chamomile flowers. Pour along with ½ cup soy oil into a sealable jar and let soak for six weeks. Shake daily. When oil turns amber, pass through a cloth and squeeze out flowers. Pour oil into a sealable bottle.

Yellow sweetclover

Melilotus officinalis

■ SYNONYMS: none

PARTS USED: The herb as a whole, including the flower, is used as medicine. Its main active ingredient is cumarin but it also contains saponin, tannins, mucilage, flavonoids and essential oils.

■ MEDICINAL EFFECTS: The cumarin acts on veins, strengthening the tonus of blood vessel walls. The flavonoids have anti-inflammatory effects.

■ APPLICATIONS: Sweetclover tea is recommended primarily for curing vein problems. It prevents the occurrence of new varicose veins and hemorrhoids. Existing inflammations of the veins recede faster. A bandage drenched in yellow sweetclover decoction helps with leg ulcers. A sitz bath soothes the pain associated with hemorrhoids and the tea also fights restlessness and sleeping disorders. Eye poultices are said to reduce swellings around the eye and soothe tired, aching eyes.

> IMPORTANT NOTE
>
> **Sweetclover tea can cause headaches.**

Tea:

Pour 1 cup boiling water over 2 teaspoons yellow sweet-clover. Steep for approx. ten minutes, then strain.

Poultices:

Pour 1 cup boiling water over 2 tea-spoons yellow sweetclover. Steep for fifteen minutes, then strain. Drench a gauze or linen cloth with decoction and place on open wound.

Sitz bath:

Pour 1 quart boiling water over 5 table-spoons yellow sweetclover. Steep for fifteen minutes, then strain. Add to lukewarm water in sitz bath; bathe ten minutes per day.

Eye poultice:

Pour 1 cup boiling water over 1 table-spoon yellow sweetclover, 1 table-spoon bluebottle and 2 tablespoons English plantain. Steep for ten min-utes, then strain. Drench cotton balls in decoction and place on closed eyelids for five minutes.

Balm

Melissa officinalis

■ SYNONYMS: lemon balm, melissa, sweet balm

■ PARTS USED: The leaves are used as medicine. The main active ingredients are essential oils, citronellal, citral as well as bitters and tannins in smaller proportions.

■ MEDICINAL EFFECTS: The essential oils have an anti-convulsant effect and prevent growth of bacteria and fungi. The tannins strengthen the heart muscle and have anti-inflammatory and antibiotic effects. The bitters stimulate appetite.

■ APPLICATIONS: Regular consumption of balm tea helps with nervousness, palpitations, stress-induced headaches and loss of appetite. A balm bath is tranquilizing; enjoyed before bedtime, it helps treat sleeping disorders. A balm tincture is said to help with tension headaches, oral herpes and athlete's foot.

IMPORTANT NOTE

Balm reproduces well in the garden or in a flowerpot in sunny places. Freshly plucked, the leaves make a refreshing tea in summer. Prepare iced tea by mixing with black tea and ice cubes.

TEA:

Pour 1 cup boiling water over 3 teaspoons balm leaves. Steep for ten minutes, then strain. Drink 3 cups over the course of the day, over a period of four to six weeks.

BATHS:

Boil 10 tablespoons balm leaves in 1 quart water. Steep for ten minutes, then strain. Add decoction to bathwater and bathe for ten to 20 minutes.

TINCTURE:

Pour ½ cup vodka over 4 teaspoons balm leaves. Soak for two weeks in a warm, dimly lit place. Strain and squeeze out residue. Keep well-sealed in an opaque bottle. For headaches, rub into temples; for oral herpes, apply to lips several times per day. For athlete's foot, apply to feet several times per day.

Mint

Mentha piperita

■ SYNONYMS: peppermint, American mint, true mint

■ PARTS USED: The mint leaves are used. Their active ingredients are essential oils, in particular menthol, flavonoids and (in smaller proportions) bitters and tannins.

■ MEDICINAL EFFECTS: The essential oils are slightly anticonvulsant and stimulate production of bile. The menthol is cooling and soothes pain. The bitters and tannins stimulate digestion and increase appetite.

■ APPLICATIONS: Peppermint tea is said to help with gall-bladder maladies. We recommend against the tea if one suffers from gastric ulcers, as the tea can irritate mucous membranes and cause an over-acidic stomach. While peppermint tea is the most popular for colds and indeed has an anticonvulsant effect, the menthol may be too strong for irritated mucous membranes; therefore, peppermint tea may actually be the wrong choice for a mucolytic remedy. However, a cup of peppermint tea does help with general indigestion from fatty foods, poor appetite, menstrual pains and nausea. Used externally, mint oil or a mint tincture can be applied for tension headaches or swellings; as it cools, it stimulates blood circulation and refreshes.

MINT **157**

TEA:

Pour 1 cup boiling water over 2 teaspoons dried mint. Steep for five to seven minutes, then strain.

TINCTURE:

Pour ½ cup brandy over 5 teaspoons mint and soak for two weeks in a warm, semi-lit place. Strain and squeeze out residue. Keep well sealed in an opaque bottle. Rub temples with tincture when suffering from headaches.

OIL:

Finely chop 6 to 10 tablespoons fresh mint and mix with ½ cup oil. Soak for four weeks in a dark place; strain and pour into an opaque, sealable bottle. Rub temples with tincture when suffering from tension headaches, or massage gently into swollen areas.

INHALATION:

In a bowl, pour hot water over 3 teaspoons dried mint (or a few drops of mint oil); inhale for ten minutes under a towel.

IMPORTANT WARNING

In nurslings and small children, the mint oil and mint tincture should not be used on faces, neck and nape. The concentration of menthol may be too strong and cause choking.

Watercress

Nasturtium officinale

▬ SYNONYMS: none

▬ PARTS USED: The whole plant (except the roots and seeds) is used. The main active ingredient is the mustard oil glycoside gluconasturtin. When fresh, watercress is rich in vitamin C and provitamin A and contains significant amounts of potassium and ferric iron.

▬ MEDICINAL EFFECTS: Gluconasturtin has antibiotic effects without affecting the intestinal flora. The vitamins invigorate the body's defenses; potassium is mildly diuretic.

▬ APPLICATIONS: Fresh watercress is used in salads or juices during spring detoxing as a refreshing "upper." Tea is recommended for coughs and bronchitis as well as for urethritis and cystitis. When dried, the herb loses its curative powers.

IMPORTANT NOTE

Do not eat more than 6 teaspoons fresh watercress per day – excess consumption may irritate the stomach lining.

Cheese spread with watercress:

Chop 6 teaspoons fresh watercress finely. Mix with 8 table-spoons low fat curd cheese and 2 tablespoons Crème Fraîche. Season with salt and pepper. The ideal spread on dark, whole-grain bread.

Watercress as a condiment:

In spring, try adding fresh, young watercress to salads or soups: it lends the meal a hint of spiciness. A daily ounce over four weeks makes a good detoxing regimen.

Nigella seed

Nigella sativa

■ SYNONYMS: black onion seed, gith (Note: nigella seeds are commonly – and falsely – called black cumin)

■ PARTS USED: The seeds are used. The active ingredients are essential and fatty oils, tannins, bitters and saponins.

■ MEDICINAL EFFECTS: The essential oil nigellone helps with bronchial spasms and essential oil thymochinone is said to stimulate secretion of bile. Gamma linolenic acid, which can be used both internally and externally, is said to alleviate skin diseases, gout, rheumatism and autoimmune deficiencies.

■ APPLICATIONS: Drinking nigella seed tea stimulates the flow of bile and prevents flatulence. Season heavy foods with black onion seed to stimulate the production of digestive fluids and to increase salubriousness. While nigella seed is not related to caraway, it stimulates – like anise and fennel – secretion of breast milk and is thus recommended for women in childbirth with lactation deficiencies. Nigella seed oil is said to reduce symptoms associated with rheumatism, gout and autoimmune diseases. Use nigella seed oil externally on dry, scaling areas of skin, e.g. neurodermatitis, gout or rheumatism.

TEA:

Pour 1 cup boiling water over 1 teaspoon crushed nigella seeds; steep for ten minutes, then strain. Drink 1 cup onion seed tea before meals.

NIGELLA SEED PACK:

Crush 5 tablespoons nigella seeds in a mortar or suitable grain mill. Peel, cook and mash three potatoes and mix in the seed. Place the hot potato on aching joints, then wrap in a towel and woolen blanket and leave until pack cools. Relieves rheumatic pains.

OIL:

Take in capsules or by the teaspoon every day. Can also be used as salad oil. Massage aching joints or dry skin with nigella seed oil.

TIP

You may find inexpensive nigella seed on offer in ethnic food stores: the seeds sprinkled on pita bread are actually nigella seed.

Basil

Ocimum basilicum

SYNONYMS: common basil, sweet basil

PARTS USED: The leaves of basil are used. The major active ingredients of this herb are essential oils such as estragole, cineole, and linalool, tannins and flavonoids.

MEDICINAL EFFECTS: The essential oils and tannins fight flatulence and stomachache. Basil is said to have sudorific effects. Pharmacologists have shown that basil can stimulate and increase lactation of women in childbed.

APPLICATIONS: Basil tea is good for stomachache and causes sweating. Women in childbed suffering from lactation deficiencies may facilitate the onset of lactation by consuming basil pesto.

GARDENING TIP

You can grow basil on your own windowsill or balcony in a flowerpot. Basil needs lots of sunlight to become rich in active ingredients.

TEA:

Pour 1 cup boiling water over 1 teaspoon dried basil. Steep for ten to fifteen minutes, then strain.

REGIMEN:

A regimen for the treatment of chronic flatulence consists of 2 cups basil tea per day for one week, followed by a two-week break, followed by another week of basil tea consumption.

PESTO:

Blend together 4 oz washed basil leaves, 1 cup olive oil and 1 oz roasted pine nuts. Add 3 z grated parmesan and season with salt. Pesto bought in stores often contains garlic. This ingredient should be avoided by women in childbirth because most breastfeeding infants dislike the flavor of garlic.

Marjoram

Origanum majorana

■ SYNONYMS: sweet marjoram, knotted marjoram

■ PARTS USED: The aboveground part of marjoram is used. The ingredients are essential oils, bitters and tannins.

■ MEDICINAL EFFECTS: The essential oils have a slightly anticonvulsant effect and thus prevent bloating. The combination of oils, tannins and bitters is also mucolytic.

IMPORTANT NOTE

Daily consumption of marjoram tea may induce headaches in susceptible individuals.

APPLICATIONS: Marjoram tea is said to help with gastrointestinal problems and with maladies related to the gallbladder. The tea helps with diarrhea, flatulence and poor appetite. Marjoram ointment can be administered to infants: when suffering from a cold, applying a little ointment below the infant's nose unblocks nostrils. For flatulence, apply a little marjoram oil above the belly button and after ten to twenty minutes, flatulence should be relieved. Marjoram ointment is also recommended for nervous pains, sprains and slow-healing wounds.

TEA:

Pour 1 cup boiling water over 1 teaspoon marjoram; strain after three minutes.

OINTMENT:

Pour 2 tablespoons alcohol over 3 to 4 teaspoons marjoram powder and rest for one hour under a lid. Add 2 tablespoons butter and heat for ten minutes in bathwater; stir constantly. Strain ointment through gauze and pour into a small sealable jar. Store the preparation in the fridge and apply cold. Make fresh ointment at least every four weeks.

OIL:

Finely chop 3 to 4 tablespoons fresh marjoram and mix with ½ cup oil. Let rest in a warm place for approx. four weeks. Strain, pour into opaque, sealable bottle and massage into affected areas.

Oregano

Origanum vulgare

■ SYNONYMS: wild marjoram, winter marjoram, wintersweet

■ PARTS USED: The aboveground part of the plant is used. Essential oils, bitters and tannins are the herb's main ingredients.

■ MEDICINAL EFFECTS: The bitters and tannins alleviate flatulence and diarrhea and support secretion of body fluids. The essential oils fight stomatitis and pharyngitis, reduce coughs, and alleviate sore throats.

■ APPLICATIONS: Oregano tea helps upset stomachs and can stop diarrhea and flatulence. Gargling with oregano tea reduces toothache and inflammations of the mouth and throat. Inhaling oregano vapors and gargling with oregano tea may also help with coughs.

TIP

Real Italian pizza is seasoned with oregano. Not only does it add to the fabulous taste, but it also supports digestion – important considering the generous amount of cheese on pizza!

Tea:

Pour 1 cup boiling water over 3 teaspoons dried oregano. Steep for ten to fifteen minutes, then strain. Allow to cool before gargling. When used as antitussic tea, sweeten with honey.

Steam bath:

Mix 1 tablespoon oregano with 1 tablespoon thyme and 2 tablespoons chamomile. Pour boiling water over the mixture. Lower face over the mixture, covering head and upper body with a large towel. Inhale vapors for ten minutes, keeping eyes closed.

Parsnip

Pastinaca sativa

■ SYNONYMS: wild parsnip, yellow parsnip

■ PARTS USED: The root and the seeds are used as medicine. The seed contains primarily essential oils and the root contains provitamin A and flavonoids.

■ MEDICINAL EFFECTS: Provitamin A strengthens the immune system and supports recovery in general. The essential oils primarily support digestion and are said to help with kidney and bladder maladies as well as stomachache.

■ APPLICATIONS: The root is best understood as a particularly healthy vegetable. It can be prepared in similar ways to carrots, raw or as a side dish, as an ingredient in a casserole or in a stew. The taste is reminiscent of parsley root, celery and carrot. Similar to carrots, parsnip ought be prepared with a little fat (for example, a drop of oil or a bit of sausage) because this facilitates the absorption of provitamin A. Parsnip tea is made from the seeds. It supports digestion and is said to stimulate the kidneys and bladder. Parsnip has been rediscovered as a condiment for pickling gherkins and pumpkin and is said to make them more digestible.

IMPORTANT NOTE

Sensitive individuals may respond to larger amounts of parsnip tea with a rash, which disappears when consumption is stopped.

TEA:

Grind 1 teaspoon parsnip seeds in a mortar. Pour 1 cup boiling water over fruit. Steep for ten minutes, then strain. Drink 2 to 3 cups per day as required.

PARSNIP VEGGIE PLATE:

Brush, peel, rinse and grate 1 lb parsnip. Rinse 1 pear, remove core and cube. Finely chop 3 tablespoons walnuts. Mix in bowl. For dressing, combine 4 oz natural yogurt, 3 tablespoons olive oil and 1 tablespoon cider vinegar. Season with sugar, salt and black pepper. Mix dressing with other ingredients.

Parsley

Petroselinum crispum

■ SYNONYMS: rock parsley, garden parsley

■ PARTS USED: The leaves and the root of parsley are used. The main active ingredients are essential oils and apiol, a phenylpropane. The leaves are rich in vitamin C, provitamin A and potassium.

■ MEDICINAL EFFECTS: Apiol has diuretic and anticonvulsant effects. It supports digestion and stimulates the gastrointestinal tract.

■ APPLICATIONS: Drinking parsley tea is recommended for flushing out the kidneys and preventing kidney grit. In cases of loss of appetite, parsley tea (or parsley wine) may stimulate production of saliva and gastric juice. Parsley poultices are said to alleviate pain and swelling associated with sprains. Half an ounce of parsley per day covers the need for important vitamins.

IMPORTANT NOTE

The concentration of apiol is very high and, when consumed in larger doses, can be toxic. Apiol increases contractility of the uterus and damages the liver, heart, and kidneys.

TEA:

Pour 1 cup boiling water over 2 teaspoons chopped leaves or root. Steep for ten to fifteen minutes under a lid, then strain. Drink before meals. A proper drinking regimen requires 3 cups per day.

WINE:

Chop 1 oz fresh parsley, place in wine bottle and fill with red wine. Cork bottle and put aside for ten days, then pass through a cloth. Drink 1 liqueur glass morning and evening.

POULTICE:

Fold 1 oz fresh, chopped parsley into 1 whipped egg white. Spread onto cloth and fix on sprain using an elastic bandage.

Spruce fir
Picea abies

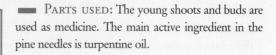

▬ SYNONYM: Norwegian spruce

▬ PARTS USED: The young shoots and buds are used as medicine. The main active ingredient in the pine needles is turpentine oil.

▬ MEDICINAL EFFECTS: Turpentine oil has anti-convulsant and mucolytic effects on the bronchial tubes. Applied to the skin, it stimulates blood circulation in connective tissue and underlying muscles.

▬ APPLICATIONS: Baths and steam baths with the pine needles help, via inhalation, alleviate colds, coughs and bronchitis. The baths stimulate blood circulation, are sudatory and help with tension pains. Rubbing the chest with a spruce tincture solubilizes the mucus in the bronchial tubes; massaging hardened muscles with a spruce tincture releases tension.

IMPORTANT NOTE

Avoid spruce tea! In the case of overdose, the mucous membranes become irritated. Do not use spruce oil for treatment of bronchial asthma and whooping cough.

Baths:

Wrap 2 handfuls fresh spruce pine needles in gauze cloth and suspend into bathwater. Of course, you may also use spruce extract from the drugstore or pharmacy. For the right dosage, consult the product information leaflet.

Steam baths:

Pour hot water over several tablespoons of fresh spruce pine needles; inhale for ten minutes under a blanket.

Tinctures:

Pour ½ cup pure alcohol (available in pharmacies) over 3 tablespoons fresh spruce shoots and pine needles. Let this infusion steep in a sealable container for ten days, then strain and dilute 1:2 with water. Keep in a sealable sterile bottle. Rub your chest with this tincture to treat mucous bronchial tubes or hardened muscles to release tension.

Massage oil:

Pour 1 cup olive oil over 3 tablespoons fresh spruce shoots and pine needles. Allow mixture to soak for four weeks. Strain and keep in a sealable bottle. Massage into hardened muscles.

Anise

Pimpinella anisum

■ SYNONYMS: aniseed, sweet cumin

■ PARTS USED: Only the small, roundish, egg-shaped fruit (known as the "aniseeds," although they are not really seeds) are used. The dried fruit contain essential oils, in particular, trans-Anethole, as their main ingredient.

■ MEDICINAL EFFECTS: The essential oils of anise alleviate flatulence and coughing and invigorate the stomach as well. Anise also supports lactation in childbed. Trans-Anethole is said to have estrogenic effects.

■ APPLICATIONS: When drunk in small quantities over the course of the day, anise tea is said to alleviate coughs and flatulence. Nursing babies may be given approx. one tablespoon of anise tea before feeding to increase appetite. Women in childbed who suffer from insufficient lactation ought to regularly drink anise tea, or special nursing teas containing anise. Rubbing anise oil on the breasts is said to also stimulate lactation.

TIP

Anise is well-tolerated even by infants. Unsweetened anise tea may be administered for newborn colic and gases, via a feeding bottle.

Tea:

Grind 1 teaspoon anise in a mortar. Add 1 cup hot water, steep for ten minutes, then strain. Sweeten with honey or sugar, as desired. For coughs, drink 2 to 5 cups over the course of the day.

Nursing tea mixture:

Have your pharmacist prepare a mixture of anise, fennel, black cumin, dill, marjoram and balm in equal quantities. Grind enough mixture for 1 portion in the mortar and pour hot water over it. Allow to steep for ten minutes, then strain.

Oil:

Grind 1 tablespoon anise in a mortar. Mix with ½ cup olive oil or black cumin oil (available at most drugstores). Allow to steep for one week in a darkened place, then strain and store at room temperature away from light. Massage oil onto breasts. Anise oil is also available ready-made at most pharmacies in combination with other lactative medicinal plants.

Burnet

Pimpinella saxifraga

■ SYNONYMS: lesser burnet, salad burnet

■ PARTS USED: The root – which contains essential oils, phenyl ester epoxides, tannins, saponins, poly-acetylenes and cumarins – is used.

■ MEDICINAL EFFECTS: Phenyl ester epoxides highly enhance secretion and have a strong anti-inflammatory effect. Burnet is thus an effective therapeutic agent for inflammations of the upper airways.

■ APPLICATIONS: Burnet tea is used in gargles for strep throats, bronchitis and coughs or it can be sipped in cases of indigestion or lack of appetite. The root is also recommended for treatment of gout, kidney or bladder stones, menstrual problems and nervous palpitation; however, there is no scientific proof of such effects as of yet.

IMPORTANT NOTE

Burnet is easily mistaken for other umbelliferae. We therefore strongly advise against digging for roots; rather, purchase burnet at a pharmacy.

TEA:

Pour 1 cup cold water over 1 teaspoon dried burnet root. Bring to a boil and let simmer at low temperature for three minutes before straining. Gargle 3 times per day with lukewarm tea or drink 3 cups per day in small sips.

MACERATION:

To make a gargle for treatment of stomatitis and pharyngitis, steep 2 teaspoons dried root in 1 cup water for one day.

English plantain

Plantago lanceolata

■ SYNONYMS: ribwort, jackstraw

■ PARTS USED: The leaves of English plantain are used. Their most important active ingredients are mucilage, tannins silicic acid, flavonoids and the glycoside aucubin .

■ MEDICINAL EFFECTS: Aucubin has antibiotic properties. The tannins help to kill harmful bacteria in mucous membranes and mucilage protects mucous membranes from germs. The silicic acid is rich in silicon, which is needed for building mucous membranes, cartilage and bone tissue. The flavonoids have an anti-inflammatory effect.

■ APPLICATIONS: English plantain tea is excellent for coughs. Also popular is English plantain syrup, which is administered primarily to children. Gargling with an English plantain preparation is recommended for stomatitis and pharyngitis. Fresh leaves, lightly crushed, can be placed on inflammations, itchy skin and insect stings.

TIP

If you are trying to quit smoking, regular consumption of English plantain tea can possibly help you succeed. No explanation for this effect has been found yet, but many ex-smokers insist the tea helped them kick the habit.

Tea:

Pour 1 cup boiling water over 2 teaspoons dried English plantain; steep for ten minutes, then strain. Drink 2 to 3 cups over the course of the day. Sweeten with honey.

Syrup:

Pour 1 cup boiling water over 1 handful fresh or dried English plantain. Cool, strain and squeeze out residue. Reheat to boil and reduce to half the amount on a medium flame. Stir in ¼ cup honey until dissolved and pour into a sterile bottle while still warm. Consume by teaspoon several times per day, as needed.

Knotweed

Polygonum aviculare

■ SYNONYMS: goose grass, bird weed

■ PARTS USED: The aboveground part of the plant is used, and its main active ingredients are silicic acid, mucilage, tannins and flavonoids.

■ MEDICINAL EFFECTS: The silicic acid contains silicon, which contributes to the formation and strenghtening of cartilage, bones, and connective tissue. The tannins help to kill harmful bacteria in mucous membranes. The mucilage protects mucous membranes against germs. Flavonoids in combination with the silicic acid stimulate urination.

■ APPLICATIONS: Knotweed tea is recommended for coughs and ailments of the respiratory tract. For stomatitis and pharyngitis, drinking small sips or gargling with the tea is recommended. When used therapeutically, knotweed tea is said to be diuretic and is thus recommended for a spring detox or for gout and rheumatism. Knotweed poultices can be used for leg ulcers and chronic wounds.

TIP

You will not find knotweed at most pharmacies - it has gone somewhat out of fashion in recent years. However, you can collect and dry it yourself, as it is abundantly widespread. It is best collected during bloom. Dry it bundled in sheaves, suspended in a shadowy place.

TEA:

Pour 1 cup boiling water over 2 teaspoons dried knotweed. Steep for ten minutes, then strain. Allow to cool if intended as a gargle. If used as a tea for coughs, sweeten with honey.

TEA MIXTURE FOR A TEA REGIMEN:

Mix 2 teaspoons dried knotweed with 2 teaspoons dried birch leaves. Pour 1 cup boiling water over the mixture. Steep for ten minutes, then strain. Drink 3 cups per day over the course of four weeks.

POULTICES:

Pour 2 cups boiling water over 4 tablespoons dried knotweed. Steep for ten minutes, then strain. Drench a linen or gauze cloth in decoction and place for 20 minutes on affected area. Repeat several times per day.

Silverweed

Potentilla anserina

■ SYNONYMS: wild agrimony, goosewort

■ PARTS USED: The aboveground part of the plant is used as medicine. The main active ingredients of silverweeds are flavonoids and tannins.

■ MEDICINAL EFFECTS: The flavonoids have anticonvulsant effects and the tannins prevent growth of certain bacteria and fight diarrhea.

■ APPLICATIONS: The tea helps with diarrhea. If consumed regularly before the expected date of menses, it soothes abdominal cramps. Infant colics, as well as gastrointestinal

cramps, are alleviated with silverweed tea. Gargling with silverweed tea is said to have a positive impact on the healing process of stomatitis and pharyngitis.

TEA:

Pour 1 cup boiling water over 1 teaspoon dried silverweed; steep for ten minutes, then strain. Drink regularly as needed. Cold or lukewarm, the tea can also be used for gargling.

Administer 3 teaspoons unsweetened silverweed tea to infants prior to breastfeeding. For bottle-fed infants, place 3 tablespoons unsweetened silverweed tea into formula.

TEA MIXTURE:

Mix 1 teaspoon dried silverweed, 1 teaspoon dried balm and 1 tablespoon dried peppermint. Pour 1 cup boiling water over the mixture; steep for ten minutes, then strain. This tea is less bitter and tastes better than tea made from silverweed alone.

IMPORTANT NOTE

Do not drink more than 3 cups of silverweed tea per day, as consuming higher doses may damage the liver.

MILK:

Boil 2 teaspoons dried silverweed with 2 cups milk; steep for five minutes, then strain. Season with honey and cinnamon. Alleviates menstrual pains.

Tormentil

Potentilla erecta

SYNONYMS: bloodroot, English sarsaparilla

PARTS USED:
The root of tormentil is ground to a powder and is exceptionally rich in tannins, especially catechines.

MEDICINAL EFFECTS: The tannins are antiseptic and astringent.

> **TIP**
>
> Consult your physician if diarrhea continues for more than days after consuming tormentil tea.

APPLICATIONS: Stomatitis, pharyngitis and tonsillitis may be treated effectively by gargling tormentil tea. Tormentil tea can also stop diarrhea. Washing with tormentil or using compresses helps burns, frostbite, hemorrhoids or slow-healing wounds.

Tea:

Pour 1 cup hot water over 1 teaspoon tormentil powder and steep for ten minutes, then strain. Can be ingested or used for gargling.

Baths:

Dissolve 1 tablespoon tormentil powder in water and bathe affected body part for five to ten minutes.

Poultices:

Mix tormentil powder with a small amount of water or curd cheese. Stir. Spread the paste onto a bandage and place on wound. Remove after 30 minutes.

Primrose

Primula veris

■ SYNONYMS: cowslip

■ PARTS USED: The root and flowers are used as medicine. The main active ingredients are saponins, in addition to flavonoids, essential oils, tannins and silicic acid.

■ MEDICINAL EFFECTS: The saponins stimulate the stomach lining and the reflux, governed by the autonomic nervous system. This increases lung secretion and facilitates expectoration.

■ APPLICATIONS: Primrose tea is used especially for colds accompanied by dry coughs, but is also recommended for gout, rheumatism, migraine, a weak heart, insomnia or anxiety attacks.

IMPORTANT NOTE

Certain persons may respond with a local allergic reaction upon skin contact with primrose. These persons must not drink primrose tea.

TEA:

Pour 1 cup cold water over 1 teaspoon dried primrose root or flower. Boil and steep for five to ten minutes, then strain. Drink 3 to 4 cups per day.

TEA MIXTURE:

Crush 1 teaspoon dried primrose root with 1 teaspoon thyme and 1 teaspoon anise seed. Pour 1 cup boiling water over the mixture, then strain. Drink 2 cups per day.

Blackthorn

Prunus spinosa

■ SYNONYMS: sloe

■ PARTS USED: The flowers and berries (sloes) of blackthorn are used. The active ingredients of the flowers are amygdalin, cumarin derivatives and flavonglycosides. The sloes contain tannins, vitamin C, amygdalin and fruit acids.

■ MEDICINAL EFFECTS: The amygdalin, cumarin derivates and the flavonglycosides have slightly laxative and diuretic effects. The vitamin C invigorates the body's defenses and supports healing. In particular, the body requires an additional supply of this vitamin during a fever.

■ APPLICATIONS: Blackthorn leaf tea is recommended as a mild laxative for kidney stones, coughs and irregular, painful menstruation. The fruit can be turned into jelly, paste or juice. When regularly consumed, blackthorn invigorates the body's defenses.

DID YOU KNOW ...

Raw sloes can be toxic in quantity, since amygdalin is a hydrocyanic acid derivative and thus is poisonous to human beings in higher concentrations. Cooking does, however, destroy the amygdalin. The raw fruit becomes edible only after the first frost of the winter.

TEA:

Pour 1 cup boiling water over 2 teaspoons blackthorn leaves. Steep for ten minutes, then strain. Add honey and lemon juice if desired. Do not consume more than 2 cups per day.

SYRUP:

Rinse and cut into halves 1 lb sloes and let swell overnight in 2 cups water. Boil once; sieve. Sweeten with honey or pear syrup if desired. Pour syrup into sterile, sealable jars. Store in the fridge. Take 1 table-spoon per day.

JELLY:

Rinse and cut into halves 1 lb sloes and let swell overnight in 1 cup water. Boil once; sieve. Boil fruit paste with 2 cups white wine and 1½ lb jam sugar. Pour jelly into sterile jars; use daily as a spread or stir some into yogurt.

Oak

Quercus robur

SYNONYMS: common oak, English oak, tanner's bark

PARTS USED: The bark of young shoots is used. The bark possesses seven to 20 percent tannins as its main active substance.

MEDICINAL EFFECTS: Tannins are astringent and therefore anti-inflammatory. Furthermore, their astringent effect renders them useful for treatment of diarrhea.

APPLICATIONS: Oak bark tea is recommended for inflammations of the intestines and for diarrhea. A gargle from oak bark is useful against stomatitis and pharyngitis. A cotton swab saturated in lukewarm oak bark solution can be inserted into the nostril to stop nose bleeding. A sitz bath from oak bark helps with hemorrhoids, eczema and vaginal or anal infections. Oak bark powder alleviates sweaty feet.

IMPORTANT NOTE

Do not drink more than two glasses of oak bark tea per day; certain individuals may respond with an upset stomach. Likewise, avoid regular baths with oak bark, as the tannins can desiccate the skin.

TEA:

Pour 1 cupful boiling water over 1 teaspoonful crushed dried oak bark; steep for approximately 10 minutes and then strain.

GARGLE SOLUTION:

Let 3 tablespoons dried oak bark boil for around 15 minutes in 2 cups water and then strain. Gargle 3–4 times a day.

NOSE TAMPON:

Let a tampon soak in a still lukewarm gargle solution and insert it into the affected nostril. Remove after approximately 15 minutes.

SITZ BATH:

Let 3 tablespoons dried oak bark boil in 1 quart water for around 15 minutes and then strain. Pour the decoction into your sitz bath and bath for around 10 minutes. Apply on a daily basis in the morning and in the evening.

POWDER AGAINST FEET SWEATING

Mix 3 tablespoons aluminum oxide with 1½ tablespoon oak bark crushed to powder, add 2 tablespoons thyme leaves crushed to powder and 1½ tablespoon violet roots crushed to powder. Keep in a vessel that can be tightly closed. In the morning, before taking on socks and stockings, powder your feet.

Radish

Raphanus sativus

■ SYNONYMS: cultivated radish, black radish.

■ PARTS USED: The root is used as medicine. The active ingredients are essential oils, mustard oil glycosides, raphanol and vitamin C.

■ MEDICINAL EFFECTS: The sulphuric essential oils stimulate secretion of bile and support a quick recession of inflammations of the liver and gallbladder. This also prevents the formation of grit and gallstones. The mustard oil glycosides are said to have mucolytic and antitussic effects.

■ APPLICATIONS: Radish is used as medicine in the form of either juice or syrup. The treatment of gallbladder diseases requires a regimen of up to four glasses of radish juice per day over four weeks. Patients with sensitive stomachs should eat a slice of white bread first and avoid drinking radish juice on an empty stomach. Radish syrup is recommended for coughs, especially dry coughs such as whooping cough.

TIP

Regular weekly consumption of uncooked radish also prevents the formation of gallstones.

RADISH JUICE:

Brush and rinse radishes; squeeze in juice extractor. Drink freshly made, as the content of active ingredients is then the highest. Otherwise, store juice in the fridge.

RADISH SYRUP:

Brush and rinse radishes. Cut lengthwise in halves and hollow out. Pour honey into cavities and infuse for several hours. Pour the honey, now infused with radish juice, into a clean jam jar. Consume 1 teaspoon several times per day.

IMPORTANT NOTE

Avoid radishes if you suffer from gastritis, gastric ulcers, or gallstones.

Black currant

Ribes nigrum

▬ SYNONYMS: none

▬ PARTS USED: The fruit and leaves are used as medicine. The fruit are rich in vitamin C, potassium, fruit acid, pectins and tannins. The leaves contain mainly tannins, flavonoids, vitamin C and small amounts of essential oils.

▬ MEDICINAL EFFECTS: Vitamin C strengthens the body's defenses and stimulates healing; specifically, the body has an increased demand for vitamin C when suffering from a fever. The tannins alleviate diarrhea, coughs and hoarseness. Potassium is considered to have diuretic effects.

▬ APPLICATIONS: Black currant tea is recommended for edema and problems with passing water. A drinking regimen is recommended for gout and rheumatism as it can reduce the number of pain attacks. The juice is said to help with coughs and hoarseness. Diluted with water, it is also good for gargling. Tasty jellies, jams and juices that prevent colds can be prepared from the fruit. In combination with ash leaves, black currant leaves are said to make the perfect tea for cellulite. Fresh black currant berries (or freshly made black currant juice) are effective in cases of acute or chronic diarrhea.

TEA:

Pour 1 cup cold water over 1 tablespoon dried black currant leaves. Bring to boil, strain immediately. Sweeten with honey and lemon juice if desired. Drink as much as needed. Unsweetened and lukewarm or cold, this tea makes a good gargle.

TEA MIXTURE:

Mix 2 tablespoons dried black currant leaves with 2 tablespoons dried ash leaves. Pour 1 quart boiling water over the mixture. Steep for fifteen minutes, then strain. Drink over the course of the day.

JUICE:

Rinse 4 lbs black currant berries thoroughly and place in juice extractor. Cook for one hour, then sweeten with 1½ lbs sugar, honey or pear syrup and pour into sterile bottles. Store in a dark place and take 1 tablespoon several times a day, as needed.

DID YOU KNOW ...

Red currants are not considered a household remedy or medicinal plant, but are also rich in vitamin C and potassium. They have a less tart taste and are equally recommendable for making juice or jelly.

Castor-oil plant
Ricinus communis

■ SYNONYMS: Mexico seed, palma Christi

■ PARTS USED: The seeds of the castor-oil plant are used. The plant is known as a tree, shrub or annual weed, depending on the climate. The seeds contain castor oil, which is gained through either maceration or digestion.

■ MEDICINAL EFFECTS: Castor oil is a very strong laxative. Applied externally, it is used to peel away calluses and dandruff from unbroken skin, as it easily penetrates the intermediate layer.

■ APPLICATIONS: Castor oil is an extremely effective natural laxative. In contrast to other household remedies, it is recommended for acute rather than chronic constipation. Depending on the dosage and on individual predisposition, it brings about a more or less thorough defecation after two to eight hours. It is in the patient's own interest that the nearest bathroom is not too far away. Externally, the oil is recommended for dandruff, dry rashes, and extremely calloused feet.

IMPORTANT NOTE

Pregnant women, children under the age of twelve and individuals with chronic constipation or ileus (blockage of the large intestine) should avoid castor oil. That said, castor oil is used before childbirth to empty bowels and facilitate delivery. However, this should be discussed with doctor or midwife rather than tried independently.

OIL FOR CONSTIPATION:

Take 1 to 2 tablespoons castor oil. Follow up by eating bread or sucking on a piece of candy to neutralize the taste. After 2 hours, the oil brings about the desired effect.

CASTOR & AVOCADO OIL:

Mix 1 teaspoon castor oil with 1 teaspoon avocado oil and 1 tablespoon soy oil. Apply to brittle fingernails and toe-nails with a small brush. Renders the nails glossy and firm.

CASTOR & SESAME OIL:

Mix 1 teaspoon castor oil with 2 table-spoons sesame oil. After a footbath and pedicure using pumice, rub feet with oil, as it prevents formation of calluses.

Wild rose
Rosa corymbifera, Rosa canina

■ SYNONYMS: dog rose, rosehip.

■ PARTS USED: The fruits (rosehips) are used. The active ingredients are vitamin C, mineral substances, flavonoids and pectins.

■ MEDICINAL EFFECTS: Vitamin C invigorates the body's defenses and supports healing. In particular, the body requires an additional supply of this vitamin during a fever. The flavonoids have anti-inflammatory and antibiotic effects. The pectins regulate intestinal digestion.

■ APPLICATIONS: Rosehip tea is recommended for colds. Rosehip syrup may be administered by the tablespoon, especially for children during cold season. Regular consumption of rosehip jelly increases the body's defenses and can thus prevent colds.

DID YOU KNOW ...

The Swedish make a tasty soup from rosehips.

TEA:

Pour 1 cup boiling water over 2 teaspoons dried rosehips. Steep for ten minutes, then strain. Add honey and !emon juice according to taste. Consume as much as desired.

SYRUP:

Rinse 1 lb rosehips, cut into halves and allow to swell overnight in 1 cup apple juice. Boil once, then sieve. Sweeten with honey or pear syrup if desired. Pour syrup into a sterile, sealable jar. Store in the fridge and consume 1 tablespoon per day.

JELLY:

Rinse 1 lb rosehips, cut into halves and allow to swell overnight in 1 cup apple juice. Boil once, then sieve. Bring paste to boil with 1 cup sallow thorn juice, the juice of 1 lemon and 1½ lb jam sugar. Pour into sterile jars and use daily as a spread or stir into yogurt.

Rose

Rosa gallica, Rosa centifolia

■ SYNONYMS: hundred-leaved rose, cabbage rose

■ PARTS USED: The rose flowers are used. The main active ingredients are anthocyanides, essential oils and tannins.

■ MEDICINAL EFFECTS: The essential oils have a mild anti-inflammatory, mucolytic and anticonvulsant effect. The tannins are mildly astringent and desiccating.

■ APPLICATIONS: Gargles based on rose leaves alleviate minor inflammations of the mouth and throat. Rose leaf tea is recommended for colds and mild diarrhea. Rose oil and swathes with rose leaf decoction can be used externally for headaches and minor wounds.

TIP

Using rose vinegar for cosmetic purposes has a long history in the Orient and involves pouring fruit vinegar instead of oil over the rose leaves. Rose vinegar is intended for persons with mixed or oily complexions as it protects the skin's natural acid mantle, jeopardized by frequent bathing.

TEA:

Pour 1 cup boiling water over 2 teaspoons dried rose leaves and strain after ten minutes. When cold, the tea can also be used as a gargle.

POULTICES:

Pour 1 cup boiling water over 5 tablespoons rose leaves and steep for ten minutes. Drench a linen cloth with decoction and place on minor wounds or on forehead. Leave until the cloth cools. Repeat several times per day.

ROSE OIL:

Cut 1 handful freshly picked rose leaves into pieces with kitchen scissors and place in bowl. Pour 2 cups olive oil over leaves and set in a sunny place for 1 week. Strain and store oil in an opaque, sealable bottle. Massage into temples when suffering from a headache; rub into minor wounds as needed.

Rosemary

Rosmarinus officinalis

■ SYNONYMS: compass weed

■ PARTS USED: The leaves of rosemary are used. The active ingredients are essential oil, tannins, bitters, flavonoids, triterpene acid and triterpene alcohol.

■ MEDICINAL EFFECTS: The essential oils stimulate the central nervous system and blood circulation. Rosemary has anticonvulsant, bactericidal and virucidal effects.

■ APPLICATIONS: Rosemary tea serves as an excellent treatment for digestive maladies. It relieves gastric cramps and helps with intestinal and gallbladder disorders. Rosemary is also said to alleviate women's ailments such as menstrual problems, vaginal discharge or menopausal neuroses. Rosemary oil can be applied externally in the form of baths or massages to relieve exhaustion. It stimulates blood circulation in the skin, reduces pain associated with sprains and dislocations, leverages blood circulation and helps with rheumatism.

IMPORTANT NOTE

Do not use rosemary oil, tea or wine during pregnancy: they can induce contractions.

TEA:

Pour 1 cup boiling water over 1 teaspoon cut rosemary leaves. Steep for ten minutes under a lid, then strain. Consume 3 cups per day.

WINE:

Finely chop 2 tablespoons fresh rosemary leaves and place in a wine bottle. Pour 1 quart white wine over rosemary. Cork bottle and leave for one week, then strain through a cloth. Drink 1 liqueur glass morning and evening.

BATH:

Boil 4 tablespoons fresh rosemary leaves with 1 tablespoon olive oil and 1 quart water; steep for 20 minutes. Strain and add decoction to full bath. Do not administer before bedtime because the bath has a stimulating effect.

Blackberry

Rubus fruticosus

▬ SYNONYMS: bramble

▬ PARTS USED: The leaves of blackberry are used, as are the delicious fruits. The main active ingredients are tannins, organic acids, flavonoids and vitamin C.

▬ MEDICINAL EFFECTS: Tannins are mildly astringent, which makes the leaves recommendable for mild forms of diarrhea and inflammations of the mucous membranes.

▬ APPLICATIONS: Blackberry leaf tea is a popular pectoral tea and soothes irritated mucous membranes. Lukewarm or cold blackberry leaf tea is often used as a gargle for sore or strep throats. The tea is also helpful in mild cases of diarrhea and with menstrual problems. While blackberry juice is primarily a food product, it is also an effective cure for diarrhea. The leaves, placed directly on inflammations, facilitate the healing process.

> TIP
>
> Blackberry leaves are easy to collect. After picking them, allow to wilt a little before crushing lightly with a rolling pin. Sprinkle water on crushed leaves and leave to dry in a dish cloth, suspended in a warm place.

TEA:

Pour 1 cup boiling water over 1 teaspoon dried blackberry leaves. Steep for ten minutes, then strain.

TEA MIXTURE:

Prepare a 2:2:1 mixture of blackberry leaves, raspberry leaves and peppermint leaves. Pour 1 cup boiling water over 1 teaspoon tea mixture. Steep for ten minutes, then strain.

POULTICES:

Mix 8 zablespoons freshly crushed leaves with minimal amount water. Stir. Soak for 3 hours. Spread a thin layer on affected area.

Raspberry
Rubus idaeus

■ SYNONYMS: hindberry

■ PARTS USED: The fruit and leaves are used as medicine. The fruit are above all rich in vitamin C, potassium, fruit acid and tannins. The leaves contain mainly tannins.

■ MEDICINAL EFFECTS: Vitamin C invigorates the body's defenses and supports healing. In particular, the body requires an additional supply of this vitamin during a fever. The tannins prevent growth of harmful bacteria and are, in combination with potassium, especially effective for urinary infections. The tannins have astringent effects on blood vessels and, to some extent, on the intestines.

■ APPLICATIONS: Raspberry tea is recommended for ailments of the gastrointestinal tract and as a gargle for stomatitis and pharyngitis. Most pregnancy tea mixtures contain raspberry leaves. They stimulate bowel movements and are said to relax pelvic muscles. Fresh raspberries, raspberry juice, syrup and jelly are all suitable household remedies for fevers, menstrual pains and urinary infections.

DID YOU KNOW ...

Many women report that drinking raspberry tea reduces the initial labor pains of childbirth and renders contractions more effective.

TEA:

Pour 1 cup boiling water over 1 tablespoon dried raspberry leaves. Steep for ten minutes, then strain. Add honey and lemon juice according to taste. Drink as much as desired. Unsweetened and lukewarm or cold, this tea is a suitable gargle.

SYRUP:

Boil 1 quart water with 1 lb sugar. Add 6 lbs rinsed raspberries and cook mixture for five minutes. Pour syrup into jars (or pass through a fine sieve and fill sterile bottles with the juice). Keep well-sealed in  a dark and cool place and have several spoonfuls over the course of the day, as required.

JUICE:

Thoroughly rinse 6 lbs raspberries and put through juice extractor. Cook for one hour; sweeten with 1 lb sugar and honey or pear syrup. Pour into sterile bottles. Keep in a dark place and consume several spoonfuls over the course of the day, as required.

Willow
Salix

SYNONYMS: catkins

PARTS USED: The bark of the tree is used as medicine. Salicin is the primary ingredient, followed by glycosides flavonoids and tannins.

MEDICINAL EFFECTS: Salicin, which the body metabolizes into salicylic acid, is said to reduce fever, alleviate pain and reduce inflammations. The glycosides, flavonoids, and tannins enhance the anti-inflammatory effect.

APPLICATIONS: Willow bark tea is recommended for feverish colds and headaches. It is also said to relieve pain associated with rheumatism or gout.

Tea:

Pour 1 cup cold water over 2 teaspoons dried and chopped willow bark. Boil. Steep for five minutes, then strain. Do not consume more than 2 cups per day.

Tea mixture for a sweat regimen:

Mix 1 teaspoon dried and chopped willow bark with 1 teaspoon dried lime flowers, 1 teaspoon dried elder flowers, half a teaspoon of aniseed and ½ teaspoon rosemary. Pour 1 cup boiling water over the mixture; steep for fifteen minutes, then strain. Drink 2 cups per day. Remain in bed to sweat out body toxins.

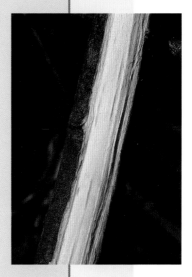

Important note

Willow bark tea should not be given to pregnant women, as it can induce bleeding.

Sage

Salvia officinalis

■ SYNONYMS: white sage

■ PARTS USED: The sage leaves, which contain a broad range of ingredients with medicinal effects, are used. The most important are essential oils, salvin, cirsimaritin and rosemaric acid.

■ MEDICINAL EFFECTS: Salvin and cirsimaritin kill bacteria. Rosemary acid has anti-inflammatory effects. The essential oils work as an anti-perspirant by influencing the brain's temperature control center.

■ APPLICATIONS: Consumption of sage tea restricts the production of sweat. Drinking two cups of sage tea per day can reduce compulsive sweating resulting from stress, anxiety, or menopause. Gargling with sage tea alleviates inflammations of the mouth and throat. The active ingredients of sage kill harmful germs, whether from simple gingivitis or a mild cough, severe tonsillitis or inflammations of mucous membranes associated with radiation therapy. Sage is also mucolytic, without desiccating mucous membranes. Sucking on sage sweets gets rid of hoarseness. Gynecologists recommend sage tea to reduce breast milk production and sage tea regulates irregular menstrual periods and relieves cramps.

IMPORTANT NOTE

Daily dosage should not exceed one-quarter of an ounce.

Nursing mothers, pregnant women and hypotonic patients should refrain from consuming sage tea regularly.

Tea:

Pour 2 cups boiling water over 2 teaspoons dried or fresh sage leaves. Steep for ten minutes, then strain. Drink 2 to 3 cups over the course of the day. When lukewarm or cold, use for gargling.

Hot sage milk:

Boil 1 teaspoon dried or fresh sage leaves with 1 cup milk; steep for three minutes, then strain. Drink 2 to 3 cups over the course of the day. This beverage is especially recommended for coughs. At night, this milk facilitates easy sleep.

Sage sweets:

Melt ½ lb sugar in a saucepan until syrupy; be careful to remove from burner before sugar gets too brown. Add 25 finely chopped sage leaves and fold into caramel. Place small heaps on greased baking paper and allow to cool.

Elder

Sambucus nigra

■ SYNONYMS: black elder, common elder, pipe tree

■ PARTS USED: The fruit and flowers are used as medicine. The fruit are rich in vitamin C, potassium, and fruit acid. The flowers contain essential oils, glycosides, flavonoids, tannins and mucilage.

■ MEDICINAL EFFECTS: Vitamin C invigorates the body's defenses and supports healing. The body requires an additional supply of this vitamin during a fever. Potassium regulates the body's water balance. The glycosides stimulate sweat glands. The flavonoids have antibiotic, mucolytic and diuretic effects.

IMPORTANT NOTE

Do not eat uncooked elderberries. The unripe fruit are mildly toxic and cause nausea.

■ APPLICATION: Elder flowers have a broad usage. Many recognize elder flower tea as a time-proven remedy for fevers because of its sudorific effect, which evaporates sweat, cools skin and thus reduces the fever. A tea regimen is said to eradicate edema and bladder stones. Elder vinegar is said to alleviate gout and bathing in elder flowers supposedly regulates greasy, impure skin. Elder juice is also used for influenza and colds. Like the flowers, it reduces fever, dissolves mucus and strengthens the immune system.

TEA:

Pour 1 cup boiling water over 1 tablespoon dried elder flowers. Steep for ten minutes, then strain. Consume as much as desired.

REGIMEN:

Drink at least 4 cups elder flower tea per day over the course of four weeks.

BATH:

Fill a linen pouch with two handfuls of fresh elder flowers. Suspend in bathwater and bathe for ten minutes.

JUICE:

Strip the stems from 6 lbs elderberries, rinse the berries and place in juice extractor while dripping wet. Cook for one hour, sweetening with 1 lb sugar, honey, or pear syrup. Pour into sterile bottles. Store in a dark place and consume 1 tablespoon several times per day, as needed.

VINEGAR:

Steep one handful elder flowers in 2 cups white wine vinegar in a dark place for fourteen days, then strain. Pour into sterile bottles and drink one glass per day.

Savory

Satureja montana

■ SYNONYMS: winter savory

■ PARTS USED: The whole plant when in flower, except the root. The active ingredients are essential oils, tannins, bitters, sitosterol and ursolic acid.

■ MEDICINAL EFFECTS: The essential oils have an overall positive influence on the gastrointestinal tract. Savory is also considered a good expectorant.

■ APPLICATIONS: Savory tea is said to help with flatulence, diarrhea, or a lack of appetite. Savory tea should be given to infants to alleviate coughs and whooping cough. Bathing with savory is also considered a good cure for the common cold.

> ## TIP
>
> Savory is an important condiment in your kitchen, which not only adds flavor to cooking, but is also good for your digestion.

TEA:

Pour 1 cup hot water over 1 teaspoon dried savory and steep for about ten minutes. Strain. Drink warm, sweetened with honey if desired.

BATHS:

Pour 1 quart boiling water over three bunches savory (4 ounces) and steep for 20 minutes. Strain and add to bathwater. Another bath ingredient can be made with a 1:1 mixture of thyme and savory.

Milk thistle

Silybum marianum

■ SYNONYMS: Our Lady's thistle, holy thistle

■ PARTS USED: The fruit of milk thistle are used. The main ingredient is silymarin, a complex from three flavonoids; in addition, the fruit contain essential oils and bitters.

■ MEDICINAL EFFECTS: Silymarin is said to be a hepatoprotectant. Used externally, the ingredients are said to have a soothing effect on varicose veins and ulcers of the lower leg.

■ APPLICATIONS: Milk thistle fruit are said to aid recovery from fatty liver or hepatitis, helping liver cells regenerate at a faster rate or preventing them from being destroyed in the first place. Poultices from milk thistle are said to reduce pain associated with varicose veins and facilitate healing of ulcers of the lower leg.

TIP

Some have reported that crushed seeds are also available at their local pharmacy or medical care supplier. It is claimed that this powder facilitates healing when strewn on leg ulcers.

TEA:

Pour 1 cup boiling water over 1 teaspoon milk thistle fruit, strain after fifteen minutes. Drink 3 cups tea over the course of the day, preferably on an empty stomach in the morning and as a last drink before dinner in the evening.

TEA MIXTURE:

The above tea can be improved in taste if either 1 teaspoon peppermint or 1 teaspoon ground fennel seed is added.

TEA MIXTURE FOR IMPROVING SECRETION OF BILE:

Mix 1 teaspoon milk thistle fruit with ½ teaspoon horehound, ½ teaspoon dandelion root and ½ teaspoon peppermint. Pour 1 cup boiling water over the mixture and strain after fifteen minutes. Drink 3 cups per day before main meals.

POULTICES:

Pour 1 cup boiling water over 2 tablespoons milk thistle fruit and steep for ten minutes. Immerse a linen cloth in decoction and wrap around lower leg. Cover with a towel and leave until cloth has cooled. Repeat several times per day.

Potato

Solanum tuberosum

SYNONYMS: none

PARTS USED: The plant's tuber is used. The active ingredients are mainly vitamin C and potassium.

MEDICINAL EFFECTS: Vitamin C invigorates the body's defenses and potassium stimulates the kidneys. When applied externally, the potato's capability to preserve heat is utilized.

APPLICATIONS: A simple potato soup is soothing for stomach patients and those suffering from diarrhea. During a diarrhea attack, the body loses large amounts of potassium: potato soup is rich in this mineral substance and consumption does not irritate the stomach. Each spring, the potato diet has its proponents as potatoes purify the organism and may have an anti-hypertensive effect in regimens for hypertension patients, provided that they are used in low-sodium dishes. Potatoes are also popular for externally applied remedies. The hot potato pack is used for lumbago and other painful, crampy pains of the back. A mashed potato pack is a well-tried remedy for conjunctivitis. Ground potatoes bring relief in cases of mild burns and scalds.

TIP

Potatoes make a good moisturizing mask for the skin: apply ground potatoes to clean skin and rinse after twenty minutes. Rubbing clean skin with a raw potato slice allegedly gets rid of blackheads.

POTATO SOUP FOR DIARRHEA:

Brush, rinse, peel and cube two potatoes and 1 carrot. Cook until done in half pint water for 20 minutes. Mix in blender and salt lightly.

POTATO POUCH:

In a sufficient amount of water, boil up to 10 lbs potatoes in their skins for 20 minutes or until mushy. Mash and pour into a pillowcase or linen bag. Keeping pouch as hot as tolerable, place on back. Cover with a towel and woolen blanket and leave on back until pouch cools. Remain in bed for at least another hour.

MASHED POTATO PACK:

Heat 5 tablespoons milk and mash in one hot potato in its skin. Stir in one egg yolk. Spread on bandage and leave on closed eye for 20 minutes. Repeat two to three times per day.

GROUND POTATO:

Peel one potato and grind with vegetable or cheese grater. Place ground potato with juice on a gauze cloth and leave on affected area for five to ten minutes.

Mountain ash (European)

Sorbus aucuparia

■ SYNONYM: Rowan tree

■ PARTS USED: Usually the ripe, red fruit, which contain lots of vitamin C, tannins, bitters, parasorbic acid and a small amount of essential oils are used as well as the leaves.

■ MEDICINAL EFFECTS: Vitamin C strengthens the body's defenses and stimulates the immune system. Tannins and bitters, along with the essential oils, increase appetite.

■ APPLICATIONS: Fresh so-called "rowanberries" make a good jam or paste. Rowanberry puree tastes great straight from the spoon or can be eaten as a spread. Regular consumption invigorates the body's defenses and stimulates the production of gastric juice. Tea can be made from dried rowanberries and is said to help with poor appetite, diarrhea, and upset stomach. An infusion from the leaves helps with hoarseness and strengthens the voice.

TEA:

Grind 1 teaspoon dried rowanberries in a mortar. Pour 1 cup water over fruit. Steep for ten minutes, then strain. As needed, drink 1 to 2 cups per day.

INFUSION:

Add 1 oz leaves to 1 quart boiling water; steep for ten minutes. Drink 3 cups per day.

JAM:

Pick 2 lbs rowanberries from their pedicels. Chill in freezer overnight. Cook until tender with 2 cups water until they burst. Sieve. Collect pulp in a saucepan and bring to boil with 2 lbs jam sugar. Refine with juice from two oranges and pour into sterile jam jars; seal well. This jam should remain fit for consumption for one year. If you like jelly straight from the spoon, replace jam sugar with standard sugar in preparation.

IMPORTANT NOTE

While it is true that the parasorbic acid from large amounts of rowanberries, when eaten raw, causes nausea and vomiting, true poisoning resulting from the bitter-tasting raw rowanberry is highly unlikely.

Comfrey

Symphytum officinale

▬ SYNONYMS: blackwort, bruisewort

▬ PARTS USED: The root, which contains the main active ingredients, (allantoin, mucilage, and tannins) is used.

▬ MEDICINAL EFFECTS: Allantoin improves circulation and increases cell regeneration, thus speeding up the healing process.

▬ APPLICATIONS: Comfrey poultices facilitate the healing of fractures, strain traumas, sprains and dislocations. Swelling recedes and pain is alleviated through application of comfrey-based ointment (available only from pharmacies).

IMPORTANT NOTE

Due to the pyrrolizidine alkaloids contained in comfrey, which are toxic to the liver, comfrey must not be ingested. External use should also be limited to a period of no more than six weeks. Pregnant and nursing women, as well as infants, are discouraged from using comfrey.

POULTICES:

Boil 4 oz chopped comfrey root in 1 quart water for approx. ten minutes, then strain. Make warm packs from the decoction and place them on injury. DO NOT place packs on open wounds.

Clove

Syzygium aromaticum

■ SYNONYMS: none

■ PARTS USED: The flower buds of the clove tree are used. The active ingredients are for the most part essential oils and tannins. Other ingredients are flavonoids, sterolins and fatty oils.

■ MEDICINAL EFFECTS: The essential oils and tannins act as a disinfectant in the mouth, throat and intestines. They are said to be especially effective for toothaches. Cloves are said to stimulate the stomach, soothe pain from mosquito bites and ward off insects.

IMPORTANT NOTE

Excessive consumption of clove irritates the mucous membranes to an intolerable degree. However, your taste buds will remind you where the limit is.

■ APPLICATIONS: Chewing cloves is said to help with toothache - although that does not mean you can avoid the dentist! Rather, cloves may help you soothe dental pain until you are able to see your dentist. Mosquito bites can be rubbed with clove oil, which has disinfectant effects. In the same way, you can ward off insects by applying clove oil to your skin or by placing lemon halves spiked with cloves everywhere. Clove tea helps with flatulence, mild diarrhea and poor appetite.

TEA:

Crush 1 clove in a mortar, place in cup with 1 teaspoon black tea. Pour hot water and steep for three to five minutes, then strain. Drink 1 cup of this tea before or after meals.

SPIKED LEMON HALVES:

Spike the pulp of a freshly cut lemon half with cloves: an effective remedy for driving away mosquitoes.

OIL:

Clove oil is available in pharmacies, well-stocked drug stores or in health food stores. Please read the instruction leaflet for the proper dosage.

Dandelion

Taraxacum officinalis

■ SYNONYMS: pissabed, fairy clock

■ PARTS USED: The young leaves before bloom and the roots are used as medicine. The active ingredients are bitters, triterpenes, steroles, flavonoids, tannins, potassium, zinc and group B vitamins.

■ MEDICINAL EFFECTS: The bitters increase appetite and stimulate secretion of bile. They are said to be anti-inflammatory. Potassium is diuretic and the combination of active ingredients has a positive effect on connective tissue.

■ APPLICATIONS: Dandelion tea stimulates the liver and kidneys. Bile and urine are produced at an increased rate. A dandelion tea regimen purifies and reduces pain associated with rheumatism. Rheumatic patients should also try dandelion root packs for aching joints. Dandelion tea regimens allegedly strengthen connective tissue. Young dandelion leaves make a tasty salad and are rich in vitamins and mineral substances, thus enhancing a dandelion regimen.

IMPORTANT NOTE

The white latex in the stem can lead to intoxication when consumed in large amounts. Some insist that swabbing warts with the latex eradicates them.

TEA:

Pour 1 cup cold water over 2 teaspoons dandelion; boil for one minute. Steep for fifteen minutes, then strain. For a dandelion regimen, drink 2 cups per day for at least six weeks. To support the therapy, eat one portion of dandelion salad at least once per week.

TEA MIXTURE:

Mix 1 teaspoon dandelion, ½ teaspoon blackthorn flowers, ½ teaspoon peppermint and half teaspoon viola. Drink 1 cup morning and evening for rheumatism treatment.

POULTICES:

Pour a small amount cold water over 3 tablespoons dandelion root; boil for five minutes. Mash to make paste. Spread on a linen cloth and place on aching joint. Cover with towel.

DANDELION SYRUP:

Pour 1 cup cold water over 2 teaspoons dandelion leaves and 2 teaspoons dandelion root; boil for one minute. Steep for fifteen minutes, then strain. Cook with 5 oz sugar until syrupy. Pour into a screw-top jar and consume 1 tablespoon per day.

Creeping thyme
Thymus serpyllum

■ SYNONYMS: wild thyme, mother of thyme

■ PARTS USED: The aboveground part of the plant is used. The main active ingredients are essential oils, bitters and tannins.

■ MEDICINAL EFFECTS: The essential oils have an anti-convulsant and disinfectant effect. The bitters and tannins stimulate digestion and production of gastric juice.

■ APPLICATIONS: Creeping thyme tea alleviates stomachache, reduces bloating and relieves abdominal cramps. Gargling with or sipping creeping thyme tea helps with dry coughs and whooping cough. When applied externally, a tincture of creeping thyme can alleviate painful rheumatic joints and a footbath of creeping thyme revitalizes feet after a long day of walking or standing.

> TIP
>
> Creeping thyme is closely related to thyme and can therefore replace thyme as a condiment.

TEA:

Pour 1 cup boiling water over 2 teaspoons dried creeping thyme. Steep for ten to fifteen minutes, then strain. When used for coughs, sweeten with honey.

TINCTURE:

Pour half a cup of brandy over 4 tablespoons dried creeping thyme; leave to soak in a warm, dark place. Strain and pour into an opaque, sterile bottle. Rub into aching joints several times per day.

FOOTBATH:

Mix 5 tablespoons thyme with 2 tablespoons rosemary. Pour boiling water over the mixture; steep for ten minutes. Add to bathwater. Make sure the footbath is the right temperature and bathe feet for ten to twenty minutes. Rub feet dry and apply oily foot lotion.

Thyme

Thymus vulgaris

■ SYNONYMS: common thyme

■ PARTS USED: The above ground part of the plant is used. The main active ingredients are essential oils, especially thymol, carvacrol, and zymol and tannins.

■ MEDICINAL EFFECTS: The essential oils have mucolytic and anticonvulsant as well as disinfectant properties. The tannins help to kill harmful bacteria in mucous membranes.

■ APPLICATIONS: Thyme tea is recommended for intestinal infections and indigestion. Gargling and slow sips of the tea help with diseases of the upper respiratory tract such as dry cough, whooping cough, bronchitis, tonsillitis and pharyngitis. Thyme baths and inhalations have a soothing effect for those suffering from an influenza infection with a runny nose and cough.

IMPORTANT NOTE

On rare occasions, regular gargling with thyme tea and regular baths in thyme may cause allergic reactions. Pregnant women should avoid thyme oil.

Tea:

Pour 1 cup boiling water over 2 teaspoons dried thyme. Steep for ten minutes, then strain. Allow to cool before gargling. If used as a tea for coughs, sweeten with honey.

Tea mixture for coughs and fever:

Crush 1 teaspoon dried thyme with 1 teaspoon elder flowers, 1 teaspoon dried marshmallow root and 1 teaspoon aniseeds in a mortar. Pour 1 cup boiling water over the mixture. Steep for ten minutes, then strain. Drink in small sips and remain in bed.

Vapor bath:

Pour 2 to 3 quarts boiling water over 2 tablespoons dried thyme and 2 tablespoons dried chamomile flowers. After waiting a few minutes, inhale while covering the head with a large bath towel.

Full bath:

Pour boiling water over 5 oz dried thyme; steep for one hour, then strain. Add the decoction to bathwater. Make sure the temperature is agreeable and bathe for ten to 20 minutes. Afterwards, remain in bed for at least 1 hour.

Lime

Tilia cordata, Tilia platyphyllos

▬ SYNONYMS: linden flowers, common lime tree

▬ PARTS USED: The flowers of the lime tree are used as a medicine. Their main ingredients are essential oils, flavonoids, mucilage and tannins.

▬ MEDICINAL EFFECTS: The flavonoids have an antibiotic effect. They act on the heat regulation center in the brain, activating sweat glands and the immune system.

▬ APPLICATIONS: Lime flower tea is recommended for febrile colds. The tea also acts preventatively, so it is recommended to consume some if you return home freezing cold or with wet feet. Lime flower packs are recommended for refreshing tired and dull skin. A footbath with lime flowers and leaves is said to soothe nerves.

TEA:

Pour 1 cup boiling water over 2 teaspoons dried lime flowers. Steep for ten minutes, then strain. For a sweating cure, drink 2 cups and wrap yourself into a blanket to stay warm.

TEA MIXTURE:

Mix 1 teaspoon dried lime flowers with 1 teaspoon dried rosehip, half teaspoon orange peel and ½ teaspoon elder flowers. Pour 1 cup boiling water over the mixture. Steep for ten minutes, then strain. Drink 2 cups per day.

POULTICES:

Pour 1 cup boiling water over 3 teaspoons dried lime flowers. Steep for ten minutes; strain and cool until lukewarm. Immerse a linen cloth in decoction and place on clean skin for ten minutes morning and evening.

FOOTBATH:

Mix 5 tablespoons dried lime flowers with 3 tablespoons dried lime leaves. Boil in 1 quart water; allow to cool under a lid. Decant through a sieve and squeeze out residue. Add decoction to hot footbath and bathe feet for ten to fifteen minutes.

IMPORTANT NOTE

Lime flower tea is not recommended for daily consumption, as it can unsettle the body's heat regulation.

Fenugreek

Trigonella foenum-graecum

SYNONYMS: bird's foot, Greek hay-seed

DID YOU KNOW ...

Fenugreek is a traditional condiment in Switzerland. The "Schabziger," a traditional Swiss monastic cheese, owes its distinct taste to fenugreek leaves.

PARTS USED: The dried seeds of fenugreek are used - they contain a high concentration of mucilage plus steroid saponins, sterols, flavonoids and small amounts of essential oil.

MEDICINAL EFFECTS: The mucilage is said to soften skin when applied externally. Internal use of fenugreek is said to increase peristalsis, bind cholesterol in the intestines and alleviate coughs. The seeds are also considered to have a laxative effect.

APPLICATIONS: Poultices made from a mixture of shredded fenugreek and water or vinegar are said to help with nailbed suppuration, chronic leg ulcers and boils. Shredded fenugreek in mashed food aids digestion and lowers cholesterol levels. In tea form, fenugreek is said to have antitussic and laxative effects.

Tea:

Pour 1 cup cold water over 2 teaspoons shredded fenugreek and steep for three hours. Boil and strain immediately. Drink while lukewarm; sweeten with honey (if desired).

Poultices:

Mix 4 oz shredded fenugreek seeds with water or vinegar. Stir to make a pulp. Boil. As the seeds swell and increase their volume considerably, make sure the pulp is not too thick. Spread the boiled pulp on cloth while still warm and place pack on inflammation. Leave on wound until pack is cold. Repeat three to four times per day.

Coltsfoot

Tussilago farfara

▬ SYNONYMS: foalfoot, coughwort

▬ PARTS USED: The leaves and occasionally the flowers of coltsfoot are used. The main active ingredients are mucilage, tannins, bitters and flavonoids.

▬ MEDICINAL EFFECTS: The mucilage serves as a protective layer when it attaches to mucous membranes of the respiratory and digestive tracts. The bitters tonify and increase wellbeing. The tannins starve out viruses and bacteria of mucous membranes and skin and the flavonoids strengthen the immune system and have antibiotic and anti-inflammatory effects.

▬ APPLICATIONS: Coltsfoot tea helps with dry coughs and expectoration. It has mucolytic effects. The tea is also recommended for stomatitis and pharyngitis. Coltsfoot can be used as a pack or poultice not only for pimples, blains and ulcers of the legs, but also insect stings and bites.

IMPORTANT NOTE

Coltsfoot contains pyrrolizidine alkaloids, which if consumed in high doses may lead to liver damage or even cancer of the liver. Therefore, one should not apply coltsfoot for more than six weeks per year and should not allow coltsfoot tea to steep for more than five minutes. Pregnant and nursing women should avoid coltsfoot altogether.

Tea:

Pour 1 cup boiling water over 2 teaspoons dried coltsfoot leaves. Steep for less than five minutes, then strain. Sweeten with honey and drink right after waking up in the morning. Consume up to 3 cups per day. Unsweetened, this tea is also suitable for gargling lukewarm or cold.

Pack/poultices:

Pour 2 cups boiling water over 2 tablespoons dried coltsfoot leaves. Steep for ten minutes, strain and squeeze out residue. Immerse a linen cloth in decoction and wrap around leg ulcers. Remove after ten minutes. For poor complexion, place cloth on affected area; rinse skin with cold water afterwards. Repeat procedure a second time using 2 tablespoons thyme. Apply weekly.

Facial tonic:

Pour 2 cups boiling water over 5 to 8 tablespoons dried coltsfoot. Steep for ten minutes, then strain and squeeze out residue. Pour into an opaque, sterile bottle and store in the fridge. Morning and evening, drench a cotton ball with tonic and rub on face. If tonic is applied to insect bites, swelling is reduced.

Stinging Nettle

Urtica dioica, Urtica urens

■ SYNONYMS: nettle, common nettle

■ PARTS USED: The leaves and roots are used. The main active ingredient in the leaves are flavonoids, followed by vitamin C, provitamin A, folic acid, and ferrous iron, potassium, silicic acid and amines. The roots contain tannins and a significant amount of Beta-Sitosterol.

■ MEDICINAL EFFECTS: Vitamin C and provitamin A strengthen the immune system. Folic acid and iron play a major role in treating hemopoiesis. Potassium has diuretic effects. Silicic acid strengthens connective tissue, nails and hair. Beta-Sitosterol is used in curing benign prostate carcinoma.

TIP

Do not collect nettles near roads with heavy traffic.

■ APPLICATIONS: Nettle tea is a favorite for detoxing in spring, as it flushes the kidneys free of salts, grit and stones. It strengthens the immune system and has hemopoietic effects. Nettle tea (or tea from a mixture containing nettle along with other ingredients) is also used for rheumatism. Rubbing the scalp regularly with cold tea from nettle roots is said to help with dandruff and brittle, lackluster hair. Baths are good for improving complexion. Moreover, regular consumption of nettle root tea is said to inhibit the growth of benign prostate cancer. However, this should always be discussed with your urologist first.

TEA:

Pour 1 cup boiling water over 1 teaspoon dried nettle leaves. Steep for ten minutes, then strain. Drink 3 to 4 cups over the course of the day. A drinking regimen should last at least four weeks (no longer than eight weeks) and should consist of 1 quart nettle tea per day.

NETTLE LEAVES AS AN INGREDIENT IN SALADS:

In spring, add fresh, young nettle leaves to lettuce.

HAIR TONIC:

Boil ½ lb chopped root in 1 quart water and 2 cups vinegar for half an hour. Rub into scalp once a week.

BATHS:

Pour 1 quart water over one handful nettles, boil and simmer at low temperature for two to three minutes. Steep for fifteen minutes, strain and add liquid to bathwater or use for washings.

Valerian

Valeriana officinalis

■ SYNONYMS: all-heal, capon's tail, amantilla

■ PARTS USED: The root of valerian, which primarily contains the herb's typical bitters, i.e. the valepotriates, essential oils, valeric acid and the alkaloids chatinine and valerine, is used.

■ MEDICINAL EFFECTS: The valepotriates, in combination with the essential oils, aid concentration while simultaneously producing a tranquilizing effect in response to over-excitement and nervous trepidation. The active substances influence cerebral waves and thus improve sleep disorders and sleep quality. Furthermore, the essential oils act as anticonvulsants in cases of psychosomatic, gastrointestinal problems. The alkaloids reduce heartburn and regurgitation, as they bind excess gastric acid.

■ APPLICATIONS: Tension headaches, anxiety, nervousness, and poor concentration can be treated with valerian powder and valerian tea. Valerian tinctures and valerian wine can be consumed to fight anxiety, nervousness, lack of concentration and insomnia. When added to full baths or macerated, valerian helps with falling asleep.

DID YOU KNOW...

Valerian does not actually make you tired, as is often thought; rather, it harmonizes the activity of your brain so that you can fall asleep easier at night, yet stay focused during the day. Valerian can therefore also be used to facilitate increased alertness of the body and mind.

Tea:

Pour 1 cup boiling water over 2 teaspoons dried, chopped valerian root. Steep for ten minutes, then strain. Drink 2 to 3 cups over the course of the day. Valerian is often mixed 1:1 with St. John's wort; this tea mixture has the additional power of improving one's mood. Apply regularly.

Valerian wine:

Pour 1 quart white wine over 1 oz chopped valerian root, the peel of one organic orange, one twig rosemary and one clove. Steep in a well-sealed container in a darkened place for fourteen days, then strain. Warm wine briefly before decanting into bottles. Drink one liqueur glass two to three times per day or before going to bed.

Powder:

Grind 1 teaspoon dried valerian root in a mortar and add to high-fat foods such as curd cheese, yogurt, etc.

Baths:

Let 4 oz valerian root steep in 1 quart water for ten hours. Add strained liquid to bathwater and bathe for ten minutes. Go to bed immediately afterwards.

Mullein

Verbascum densiflorum

▬ SYNONYMS: mullen

▬ PARTS USED: The flowers of mullein are used; they contain the active ingredients mucilage, flavonoids, saponins and iridoids.

▬ MEDICINAL EFFECTS: The mucilage soothes irritated mucous membranes. The saponins liquefy hardened mucus and thus facilitate expectoration and iridoids have an anti-inflammatory effect.

▬ APPLICATIONS: Mullein tea is recommended for coughs and common colds and is also said to help with diarrhea. A sitz bath or full bath is said to help with hemorrhoids and itchy skin diseases. For earaches, drip mullein oil onto a cotton swab and insert in auditory canal to alleviate pain. Repeat two to three times a day.

TIP

Mullein can be safely administered to children; however, they will most likely prefer the tea mixture for its taste.

TEA:

Pour 1 cup boiling water over 2 teaspoons mullein flowers, steep for ten minutes, then strain. Drink several cups over the course of the day.

TEA MIXTURE:

Mix 1 teaspoon mullein flowers with 1 teaspoon elder flowers and 1 teaspoon coltsfoot leaves. Pour 1 cup boiling water over the mixture, steep for ten minutes, then strain. Drink 3 to 4 cups over the course of the day.

OIL:

Pour ½ cup olive oil over one handful mullein flowers. Pour into a screw-top jar and leave in a sunny place for three to four weeks. Shake daily. Strain the oil and squeeze out flowers. Pour into an opaque bottle and use as required.

BATH:

Boil 1 quart water and two handfuls mullein flowers. Allow decoction to soak for fifteen minutes, then strain. Add this to a full bath or sitz bath.

Vervain

Verbena officinalis

■ SYNONYMS: pigeonweed, Indian hyssop

■ PARTS USED: The above-ground part of vervain is used. Its active ingredients are verbenalin, essential oils, tannins, silicic acid, bitters and mucilage.

■ MEDICINAL EFFECTS: Tannins, bitters and mucilage are said to help treat gastrointestinal problems and coughs. Used externally, they are said to soothe lumbago pains.

■ APPLICATIONS: Tea is recommended for mild forms of indigestion, diarrhea, and lack of appetite. Drinking or gargling with the tea can also soothe a sore throat and reduce coughs. A pack with vervain paste is said to reduce the pain of lumbago.

IMPORTANT NOTE

Do not mistake vervain for the tasty lemon verbena, so much sought after in the French-speaking parts of Switzerland and in France. The two plants are related, but verbena mainly contains essential oils. The lemon-scented verbena tea is said to have diuretic effects.

Tea:

Pour 1 cup boiling water over 1 teaspoon dried, chopped vervain. Steep for five minutes, then strain.

Poultices:

Chop 1 bunch fresh vervain coarsely, boil with 1 cup vinegar. Stir in rolled oats to make a puree; spread between two cloths. Place in the groin area and cover body with a woolen blanket. Allow to act on the affected area for ten to fifteen minutes.

Viola

Viola tricolor

▬ SYNONYMS: Heart's ease, trinity violet

▬ PARTS USED: The aboveground part of the plant is used as medicine, especially the flower. The active ingredients are saponins, mucilage and salicylic acid compounds.

▬ MEDICINAL EFFECTS: The saponins indirectly strengthen the immune system by facilitating absorption of other nutrients. The mucilage protects against susceptibility to harmful germs. Salicylic acid alleviates pain, has anti-inflammatory properties, and reduces fever.

▬ APPLICATIONS: Viola tea helps with dry coughs in particular and is recommended as a gargle for sore throats. The tea also helps with tension headaches and fever. A long-term drinking regimen of at least four weeks is recommended for acne or rheumatism. Nursing eczema and diaper rash are also curable with viola tea. Poultices drenched in viola decoction are recommended for eczema, acne and slow-healing wounds.

IMPORTANT NOTE

Very rarely, intensive consumption of viola tea can lead to allergic skin reactions. This undesired effect is instantly reversible by excluding the tea from one's diet.

TEA:

Pour 1 cup boiling water over 2 teaspoons viola; steep for ten minutes, then strain. Drink a maximum of 3 cups per day for at least four weeks.

TEA MIXTURE FOR TENSION HEADACHES:

Mix 1 teaspoon viola with 1 teaspoon St. John's wort and 1 teaspoon meadowsweet. Pour 1 cup boiling water over the mixture. Steep for fifteen minutes, then strain.

TEA MIXTURE FOR ACNE:

Mix 2 teaspoons viola with 2 teaspoons field horsetail; pour 1 cup boiling water over the mixture. Steep for ten minutes, then strain. Drink 3 cups per day for at least four weeks.

POULTICES:

Pour 2 cups boiling water over 4 tablespoons viola. Drench linen cloth in decoction and place on affected skin while still warm. Apply morning and evening for at least three weeks. For eczema, add the same amount of oak bark.

Ginger
Zingiber officinale

■ SYNONYMS: none

■ PARTS USED: The rhizome of the reed-like ginger plant is used. The active ingredients are mainly essential oils and spicy zingerol.

■ MEDICINAL EFFECTS: The essential oils and zingerol help with stomach problems including bloating or mild sicknesses such as travel sickness. Ginger strengthens the body's defenses and is thus an ideal remedy for colds. Like garlic, ginger is said to be an effective drug for lowering cholesterol levels and blood pressure.

■ APPLICATIONS: Ginger root has the best medicinal effects when fresh. When nauseous or suffering from travel sickness, one should chew a slice of fresh ginger or eat candied ginger. To cure a cough or cold, drink ginger tea, punch or syrup. To prevent heart attacks, use ginger regularly in cooking or drink ginger tea on a regular basis. Packs, baths and poultices prepared with a ginger decoction are recommended for alleviating muscle pains and joint pains, as these remedies have a soothing and refreshing effect. Massaging with ginger oil relaxes hardened muscles.

IMPORTANT
NOTE

Ginger does NOT alleviate pregnancy sickness.

TEA:

Peel and chop a thumb-sized piece of ginger. Cook in 2 cups water for ten to 30 minutes, then strain and sweeten with honey. If used medicinally, drink several cups over the course of the day.

PUNCH:

Prepare in the same manner as ginger tea, adding cinnamon, coriander, lemon peel and cloves before cooking.

SYRUP:

Simmer 2 teaspoons fresh, chopped ginger in 1 cup water for 30 minutes. Add 4 oz sugar or honey and cook until syrupy. Consume by the spoonful or stir into black tea.

GINGER DECOCTION:

Like the tea preparation, cook ginger for 30 minutes. Drench swathes or bandages with decoction or add strained decoction to a full bath.

MASSAGE OIL:

Juice one ginger root and mix 1:1 with sesame oil. Makes only small amounts. Stir before use. Store in the fridge.

Yogurt

■ PARTS USED: Yogurt is derived from milk through the addition of bacterial cultures, which causes the lactose contained in milk to ferment into lactic acid, which in turn causes the milk proteins to coagulate and produce a gel. At this stage, the flavor typically associated with yogurt is produced, primarily consisting of products of the bacteria's metabolism, i.e. diacetyl, acetaldehyde and various acids. When the desired pH value of approx. 4.4 is reached, stirring the milk gel prevents further acidification.

■ MEDICINAL EFFECTS: When consumed regularly, yogurt's lactic acid and related bacteria have positive effects on intestinal flora. Used externally, yogurt has a cooling effect.

■ APPLICATIONS: Regular consumption of yogurt supports healthy intestinal flora and thus prevents the onset of gastrointestinal diseases. A Finnish study concluded that cystitis in women could be prevented by regular consumption of yogurt, as pathogenic intestinal bacteria supposedly cause most bladder inflammations. Yogurt in the form of a soothing pack is also recommended for light sunburns or dandruff. Additionally, it is recommended following vaginal yeast infections to apply yogurt to the vaginal area or even to insert a tam-

TIP

Yogurt and wheat bran improve complexion. Fold approx. two tablespoons wheat bran into three to five tablespoons yogurt. Apply to the skin and let dry; rinse with lukewarm water.

pon that has been soaked in yogurt. This supports the reformation of the vagina's acidic protective layer.

TURKISH YOGURT BEVERAGE:

Mix 1 pound Turkish yogurt with 2 cups water and 1 teaspoon salt. This is a healthy beverage for quenching thirst, popular in Turkey. This mixed drink is also recommended for diarrhea.

YOGURT PACK:

Spread natural yogurt on scalp using a tablespoon and massage into skin. Leave for approx. 30 minutes or until the yogurt has dried. Wash hair and scalp thoroughly with shampoo. Apply weekly.

YOGURT VAGINAL SUPPOSITORY:

Soak a tampon in a cup of natural yogurt and then insert into the vagina. Wear a sanitary napkin and replace after two to four hours. Apply daily over a period of three to five days.

Buttermilk

■ SYNONYMS: none

■ PARTS USED: Buttermilk is a byproduct of manufacturing butter from milk. It is rich in lecithin, group B vitamins and calcium.

■ MEDICINAL EFFECTS: Lecithin and B vitamins promote healthy skin and defend the body against stressful situations. Calcium is crucial for the metabolism of bones, teeth and nails.

■ APPLICATIONS: Regular consumption of buttermilk strengthens intestinal flora and thus prevents the onset of gastrointestinal maladies. Furthermore, drinking buttermilk can fight stress and fatigue. Buttermilk can also be used externally. Bathing in buttermilk helps with mild forms of sunburn. Owing to its cooling effect, applying buttermilk to swellings and minor inflammations lessens pain and causes swelling to recede.

TIP

Rubbing in buttermilk regularly for four to six weeks is said to soften and smoothen rough skin.

Savory buttermilk shakes:

Mix 2 cups buttermilk with 6 tablespoons freshly chopped potted herbs, such as chives, parsley and basil. Season with salt and pepper. If you like carrot juice, add some to the buttermilk.

Sweet buttermilk shakes:

Mash 2 cups buttermilk with ½ lb berries, e.g. huckleberries, raspberries, strawberries or blackberries in a blender. If desired, sweeten with honey or sugar.

Baths:

Add 2 to 3 quarts buttermilk to a full bath and bathe for ten to 20 minutes. This bath moisturizes the skin and thus reduces sunburn.

Curd cheese

■ SYNONYMS: cream cheese, farmer's cheese

■ PARTS USED: Adding bacteria cultures, and sometimes a little rennin, to lukewarm milk creates curd cheese. The lactose contained in the milk is metabolized into lactic acid and causes the coagulation of lactic proteins: the curds. These are cut with a "harp." Curds and whey are separated and the latter can be drained off by pressure.

■ MEDICINAL EFFECTS: Curd cheese applied externally has a cooling effect. Curd cheese is especially rich in calcium; in combination with its low-calorie count, it is an important means of preventing osteoporosis.

■ APPLICATIONS: Regular consumption of curd cheese ensures a sufficient intake of calcium, the most important mineral substance in bone metabolism and also crucial for preventing blood clots. Used externally, curd cheese packs have a cooling effect and reduce swellings, inflammations and skin tension. Curd cheese also has a purifying and cleansing effect on inflamed skin and acne. Curd cheese packs are recommended for sore throats and for breasts irritated by the onset of lactation.

TIP

In all cases, use a low-fat curd cheese. It is far more effective than creamy curd cheese.

CURD CHEESE PACKS FOR INFLAMED EYELIDS:

Mix 3 tablespoons low-fat curd cheese with 1 tablespoon milk and a few splashes of lemon juice. Place mixture on warm, moist gauze. Place on closed eyelid for fifteen minutes. Apply twice per day.

CURD CHEESE POULTICE:

Spread a thin layer of low-fat curd cheese on inflamed area (the breast in the case of mastitis, the throat for sore throat, the elbow for chronic tennis elbow, etc.). Cover with gauze or with a dishtowel; leave until curd cheese dries and flakes off. Make this poultice several times per day until swelling, redness and heat recede.

CURD CHEESE & EGG MASK:

Mix 4 oz low-fat curd cheese with one egg. Apply mixture on face as a facial mask: leave area around the eyes uncovered and rinse off with lukewarm water after fifteen minutes. Dry and apply a moisturizing cream.

Whey

■ SYNONYMS: none

■ PARTS USED: Whey is a by-product of cheese production. When curds (coagulated milk) are separated in a centrifuge into solid and liquid components, a milky, transparent liquid (whey) drains off. It is rich in proteins, group B vitamins and mineral substances such as calcium, potassium and sodium.

■ MEDICINAL EFFECTS: Whey proteins contain amino acids essential for human nutrition, and one need not consume much to consume a healthy amount of proteins. Furthermore, whey contains high levels of group B vitamins, which are needed during periods of stress and tension.

TIP

Do not drink whey that has been "enriched" with flavors or fruit additives, as it usually contains too much sugar, which should be avoided during a fast.

■ APPLICATIONS: Whey regimens are a popular option for slimming and purification diets. Owing to the proteins' high biological valence, muscle tissue is not catabolized as fast as in many other diets.

WHEY FAST:

For one or two days per month, drink 1½–2 quarts whey in five to seven portions. A few pieces of fruit may be eaten as well. During this cure, one ought relax; therefore, these days are recommended for weekends. Quench your thirst with mineral water or herbal tea. These fasting days with whey serve primarily to purify the body.

WHEY DRINKING DIET:

The whey-drinking diet is a 10-day fasting cure, during which one consumes up to 3 quarts whey per day in several small portions. To vary the diet, one can mix unsweetened fruit juices into the whey. During this regimen, solid food is avoided.

MODERATE WHEY DIET:

Drink 1 quart whey daily over a one to 2-week period, accompanied by plentiful amounts of fruits and vegetables, as well as only low-fat wholefoods. In addition, you should drink at least 2 quarts herbal tea and water per day.

Kefir

■ SYNONYMS: milk kefir

■ PARTS USED: Kefir is made from milk containing so-called "kefir grain." Kefir grain is a symbiotic structure of lactic acid bacteria, certain lactobacillus and yeast. The lactose ferments into alcohol and lactic acid, slightly altering the structure of the milk proteins. In addition to kefir's high content of calcium and group B vitamins in general, the content of B12 vitamins is proportionally higher compared to other dairy products.

■ MEDICINAL EFFECTS: Lactic acid bacteria improve digestion. Calcium warrants healthy bone metabolism, and the B vitamins and B12 vitamin strengthen the nerves in times of stress and tension.

■ APPLICATIONS: Kefir may enjoy the resounding sobriquet "beverage of the centenarians" in the Caucasian mountains where it originates, but one should not rely on the reward of long life for drinking kefir regularly. Some claim that the regular consumption of kefir offers protection from tuberculosis and cancer, but such statements must be taken with a grain of salt. However, it is known that drinking kefir regularly strengthens and stabilizes intestinal flora and if a diet is otherwise balanced, life expectancy can be said to

TIP

Do not mistake milk kefir for water kefir. The later is made from water, dried fruit, and sugar, and is, not unlike kombucha, widely used in Far Eastern alternative medicines.

increase. A popular remedy for sunburn is to spread kefir on the inflamed skin. This has a cooling effect and prevents overheating. Bathing in kefir is also said to reduce the consequences of sunburn.

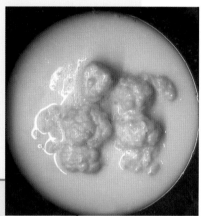

SWEET KEFIR SHAKE:

Mix 1 cup kefir with juice of two squeezed oranges. Sweeten with honey if desired. Of course, kefir can be mixed with other fruit juices as well. Drink at least one half-pint per day.

SPICY KEFIR SHAKE:

Mix 1 cup kefir with half a cup carrot juice and 3 tablespoons chopped broad-leafed parsley. Alternatively, peel, seed and mash 7 oz cucumber and mix with 1 cup kefir and 4 tablespoons dill. Season with salt and pepper.

BATH:

Add 3 quarts kefir to bathwater and bathe for 20 minutes. Rinse body and apply lotion after drying off.

Salt

■ SYNONYMS: medicinal salt, sea salt, solar salt

■ PARTS USED: Salt consists of sodium and chloride. Furthermore, it can contain other mineral substances and trace elements such as iodine, magnesium, bromine and other inorganic substances.

■ MEDICINAL EFFECTS: Salt retains water and has disinfectant and purifying effects. All fluids of the human body contain salt. By enriching water with salt, isotonic, hypotonic or hypertonic solutions can be prepared. Isotonic solutions are used in transfusions, hypotonic solutions quench the thirst, and hypertonic solutions dehydrate the body and are usually used only externally.

■ APPLICATIONS: Saltwater can be used for colds - either by inhalation, nose rinsing or gargling. It is a mild disinfectant that humidifies and reduces irritations. Bathing in saltwater is also recommended to help remove excess water from the body, e.g. during pregnancy, in a short amount of time. Saltwater makes it easier to peel off scabs and remove dandruff. A little salt on one's toothbrush is sufficient for proper dental hygiene.

SALTWATER INHALATIONS:

Dissolve 2 to 3 tablespoons salt in 2 quarts hot water; pour into a shallow dish and lower head over dish, covering with a large bath towel. Breathe vapor for ten to twenty minutes. This helps with influenza infections involving headache or blocked nose.

GARGLE / NOSE RINSING:

Dissolve 1 teaspoon salt in 1 quart lukewarm water. Using a nasal applicator, allow a small amount of saltwater to flow gently into one nostril. Helps with a blocked nose. Nose rinsing is also said to bring short-term relief to hay fever and other pollen-related allergies. Saltwater in the above concentration is also good for gargling if you have a sore throat.

BATHS:

Usually, salt from the Dead Sea or bath salts are recommended. In theory, though, kitchen salt should do the trick as well. Put half a pound to a pound of salt in a full tub of warm water. Bathe for 20 minutes and rinse body thoroughly under clear water.

TIP

Many people, especially young women, suffer from hypotension due to the fact that their diet contains too little salt and not enough water - because of their fear that salt would intolerably increase their blood pressure. In reality, however, there are only a few patients who are truly sensitive to sodium and who should monitor their salt consumption.

Sauerkraut

■ SYNONYMS: pickled cabbage

■ PARTS USED: Sauerkraut is fermented white cabbage or "pointed cabbage." The leaves are finely grated and pressure-fermented in brine. During fermentation, lactic acid bacteria are produced. The main active ingredients are lactic acid (and its bacteria culture), vitamin C and group B vitamins.

■ MEDICINAL EFFECTS: The vitamin C invigorates the body's defenses. Finnish nutritionists recently discovered cancer-halting isothiocyanates, which are produced during the fermentation of cabbage. Sauerkraut is said to stimulate the immune system and to regulate digestion.

■ APPLICATIONS:
Sauerkraut juice on an empty stomach helps with constipation and stimulates the intestines. Regular consumption of uncooked sauerkraut strengthens the body defenses and can thus prevent colds and other minor infections.

TIP

When shopping for sauerkraut, check whether it has been pasteurized. Heat destroys important ingredients and reduces sauerkraut's effectiveness.

SAUERKRAUT REGIMEN:

Over three to four weeks, consume approximately ½ lb uncooked sauerkraut per day. It is crucial not to heat the sauerkraut or to or use pasteurized sauerkraut. In order to make the regimen more tolerable, you can mix the sauerkraut with other foods and serve it as raw veggies, juice or stirred into a hot broth.

SAUERKRAUT JUICE:

To treat acute constipation with sauerkraut, it is important to drink the juice on an empty stomach. A small glass will usually suffice.

Dried fruit

■ USED PARTS/CONSTITUENTS: Dried figs, prunes, dates, or apricots (among others) are soaked in water. Dried fruit are rich in potassium, secondary plant ingredients, fibers and fructose.

■ MEDICINAL EFFECTS: The combination of fructose, fibers, and potassium stimulates bowel movements. The feces become softer and the constipation is cured.

■ APPLICATIONS: Dried fruit soaked in water relieves constipation. Juices from dried fruit (available in natural food stores or in the natural food section of your supermarket) have the same effect. However, consuming too much dried fruit (which some choose as a substitute for sweets while on a diet) can lead to diarrhea. The calorie count of dried fruit is often underestimated too - so don't be surprised if your weight remains the same after replacing sweets with dried fruit.

DID YOU KNOW ...

Consuming fresh, ripe figs on an empty stomach is an excellent remedy for constipation.

SOAKED DRIED FRUIT:

Pour some lukewarm water over three to five dried prunes and one to two dried figs. Soak overnight and consume fruit, along with the water, on an empty stomach the next morning.

Sheep's wool

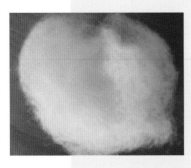

SYNONYMS: none

PARTS USED: This is natural sheep's wool that has only been rinsed with water. For this reason, it is rich in lanolin, the natural wool fat.

MEDICINAL EFFECT: The wool fat supposedly activates the body's self-healing abilities and is distributed by the large surface area created by the fine fiber tips of the wool.

APPLICATIONS: The sheep's wool can be placed on affected areas in cases of hardened muscles in the back of the neck, damaged and painful intervertebral disks, lumbago, earache, inflamed nipples, leg ulcers or diaper rash. Sheep's wool swathes on the chest or back are also said to alleviate pain associated with bronchitis. A large piece of sheep's wool placed on the abdomen supposedly brings relief to gastrointestinal cramps and baby colic.

Padding / swathe for weeping wounds:

Cut from fleece a thin layer of wool the size of wound; place on wound. Do NOT put ointment on wound beforehand. Depending on how much the wound oozes, replace wool every three to six hours. For hygienic reasons, dispose of the used padding immediately after use.

Wrapping for internal diseases:

Tear a fair-sized piece of wool from the fleece and place on the affected area. Secure with a tight T-shirt or a loose gauze bandage. Replace

the wool every morning and evening. A wool dressing may be reused if well-aired. Often, an application as short as 20 minutes can bring therapeutic benefits.

Ear swab:

For earache, form a loose ball from wool as you would from cotton and insert into auditory canal. Replace at least two to four times per day.

Water

■ SYNONYMS: medicinal water (internal use), Kneipp water therapy (external use)

■ PARTS USED: Kneipp water therapy originated in Germany, where water must meet strict requirements before it may be labeled medicinal water. Like natural mineral water, medicinal water for use in Kneipp therapy must be pristine spring water from subterranean springs, bottled at the point of origin, and must contain the original amounts of valuable mineral substances and trace elements – all of which must be declared on the label. There are over 70 official brands of medicinal water in Germany!

■ MEDICINAL EFFECTS: Dissolved carbon dioxide stimulates the digestion. The high concentration of potassium stimulates the enzymatic and nervous systems and keep the cardiovascular system in good order. The hydrogencarbonate reduces blood and urine acidity and can prevent the crystallization of urinary stones. Hydrogencarbonate also neutralizes excess amounts of gastric acid. Medicinal waters rich in calcium are a perfect preventive tool against osteoporosis. Medicinal waters rich in fluoride ensure sufficient fluoride levels in the saliva and thus prevent dental caries.

■ APPLICATIONS: Medicinal water is best consumed at room temperature. Drink at least three cups per day – there is

THE KNEIPP PRINCIPLE

"As much heat as necessary, as much cold as possible!"

no upper limit. Medicinal waters can only reap benefitial health effects if consumed daily over a long period of time.

AFFUSIONS FOR THE KNEE, BACK OF THE NECK, AND THIGH:

Knee: Direct cold stream of water from the toes to the back of knee and inner side of leg. Stimulates the blood circulation and helps with varicose veins.
Back of neck: Direct cold water from hand to back of neck via arm and shoulder. Repeat for both sides of body. Loosens hardened muscles in shoulder and back of neck.
Thighs: Direct cold water from toes along the outer side of leg and inner side of the leg. Repeat for both sides of body. Stimulates blood circulation and is good for vein problems and varices.

WATER-TREADING:

Wade into calf-deep water, either treading for ten minutes in water cooled to 55°F or alternating cold and warm water for five minutes each. Stimulates blood circulation and refreshes.

KNEIPP SHOWERS / HOT-COLD SHOWERS:

Always begin with warm water and finish with cold water. Switch between hot and cold several times to resolve sleeping disorders and hypotension.

Urine

■ SYNONYMS: water, pee, weewee

■ PARTS USED: The first urine of the morning is used; specifically, mid-stream. Its physiological contents are hormones and their various decomposed products, enzymes, vitamins, mineral substances, uric acid, urea, antibodies and antigens. The ingredients and their concentration vary depending on diet.

■ MEDICINAL EFFECTS: Scientist do not agree on the efficacy of urine therapy. Established medicine dismisses auto-urine therapy, while many schools of natural medicine use it. The philosophy behind their approach is that the morning urine contains beneficial substances that only the body itself can produce for fighting its own diseases. Urine is said to have anticonvulsant and analgesic effects, regulate and activate the hormonal system and stimulate the immune system.

■ APPLICATIONS: Urine can be used both internally and externally. Auto urine therapy is recommended for hormone disorders, disorders of the immune system (such as allergies, hay fever, urticaria and auto-aggressive diseases), inflammatory skin diseases, metabolism disorders such as rheumatism or gout, diseases of blood vessels, migraines and infectious diseases. Time and again, the external use of urine is recommended for warts, neurodermatitis and herpes zoster. Reports abound from people who have had positive experiences with urine therapy. For a long time, urine was also a widely used component of dental care, due to its ammonia content – ammonia cleans and whitens teeth.

URINE AS WART THERAPY:

When first passing water in the morning, collect urine mid-stream in a cup. Dab urine on warts with a cotton swab. Repeat daily with fresh urine.

SWATHE FOR HERPES ZOSTER:

When first passing water in the morning, collect urine mid-stream in a cup. Moisten a linen cloth with urine and place on affected area for five to ten minutes.

RUBDOWN FOR NEURODERMATITIS:

When first passing water in the morning, collect urine mid-stream in a cup. Drench a cotton ball in urine and dab raw, inflamed skin.

Vinegar

■ SYNONYMS: none

■ PARTS USED: Vinegar is fermented alcohol; as such, it may develop spontaneously; for example, if you leave an uncorked bottle of wine around long enough, bacteria will convert the alcohol into acetic acid.

■ MEDICINAL EFFECTS: Acetic acid promotes the secretion of gastric juices. It serves as a disinfectant and has cooling effects, owing to its quick evaporation.

■ APPLICATIONS: Vinegar supports the secretion of digestive juices and thus prevents bloating and flatulence. Gargling with a vinegar solution is said to protect mucous membranes in mouth and throat, due to its disinfectant effect and the fact that acetic acid stimulates salivation, which in turn promotes healthy oral flora. Drinking regimens involving vinegar are recommended for strengthening mucous catarrh, since vinegar has particularly strong expectorant powers. Dab insect bites with vinegar to alleviate pain and reduce swelling. Vinegar bread can help remove corns.

ACETIC MILK FOR CONSTIPATION:

Mix 2 tablespoons cider vinegar with 2 tablespoons water. Add to half glass milk and drink in the morning on an empty stomach.

VINEGAR BREAD:

Soak 1 slice white bread in vinegar. Apply bread pulp to corns and cover with gauze. Secure on foot using a sock and wear overnight. Repeat daily for approx. one week to remove the corn.

FOOTBATH FOR SWEATING FEET:

Mix 3 tablespoons rosemary needles with 3 tablespoons marigold (calendula) flowers. Pour 1 cup boiling water over the mixture, let cool, then strain. Mix decoction with 3 tablespoons vinegar. Pour liquid into cold footbath; bathe feet for ten to fifteen minutes. Afterwards, apply lotion and keep feet warm with woolen socks.

IMPORTANT NOTE

You can find recommendations for so-called "vinegar essence," an artificially manufactured solution of acetic acid with a concentration equal to that of natural vinegar several times over. Therefore, vinegar essence must always be heavily diluted before consumption. Better to steer clear of vinegar essence: forgetting the necessary dilution can lead to internal burns.

Index of Health Problems

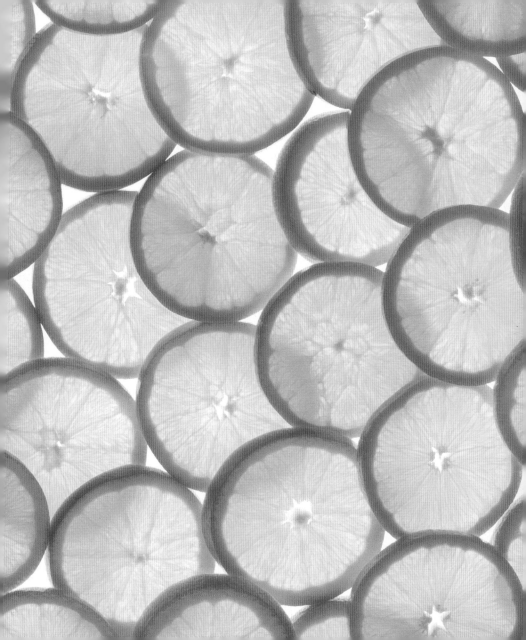